Exit Strategies for Covered Call Writing

presents

Exit Strategies for Covered Call Writing

Making the Most Money when Selling Stock Options

ALAN ELLMAN

Exit Strategies for Covered Call Writing
Making the Most Money when Selling Stock Options

www.TheBlueCollarInvestor.com

Published by Wheatmark®
610 East Delano Street, Suite 104
Tucson, Arizona 85705 U.S.A.
www.wheatmark.com

Publisher's Cataloging-In-Publication Data
(Prepared by The Donohue Group, Inc.)

Ellman, Alan.
  The Blue Collar Investor presents exit strategies for covered call writing : making the most money when selling stock options / by Alan Ellman.

   p. : ill. ; cm.

  Includes bibliographical references and index.
  ISBN: 978-1-60494-253-8

1. Finance, Personal. 2. Investments. 3. Investment analysis. 4. Stock options. I. Blue Collar Investor (Firm) II. Title. III. Title: Exit strategies for covered call writing : making the most money when selling stock options

HG179 .E44 2009
332.024   2009921866

REV201101SD

"An investment in knowledge always pays the best interest."
Benjamin Franklin

My mission was to educate myself to invest in the stock market and achieve financial freedom. I soon learned that I was not alone. This book is dedicated to Blue Collar Investors all over the world in pursuit of these same goals.

Contents

Appendix

Preface

I have been using the strategy of selling covered call options for more than ten years. I was never specifically advised to utilize covered call writing as my primary investment strategy. Those who read my first book, *Cashing in on Covered Calls[1]*, know that when I first started the process of self-education in the stock market two decades ago, of the many different investment strategies I studied, covered call option writing particularly caught my attention, not only because of the high returns it enabled me to generate, but also because of the unique tax benefits the strategy offered. Focusing on this strategy, and after years of self-education and trial and error, I ultimately was able to develop a covered call writing strategy that generated returns far greater than those that otherwise could have been derived by simply buying and selling stocks, exchange-traded funds (ETFs), or mutual funds. It is these techniques that I have developed within this investment approach; techniques that I have refined for over a decade and which I have been unable to find in books or other media entities; that I know you, the Blue Collar Investor, can master.

I can attest to the validity of the statement "success breeds excitement and motivation." The more I saw my strategy generating great returns, the stronger my thirst developed for even more success. Even

---

1   Alan Ellman, *Cashing in on Covered Calls* (SAMR Productions, 2007).

more stimulating was the fact that others wanted to learn what I was doing and how I was doing it. This groundswell of interest inspired me to write a seminar series (now on DVD and CD) and the penning of my first book referenced above. In addition, I have also created a website, **www.thebluecollarinvestor.com**, where I regularly publish journal articles on my blog and receive daily commentary and valuable insight from other Blue Collar Investors throughout the world who also have found success utilizing my strategies.

The feedback from The Blue Collar Investor Series has, in no small way, changed my life. Investors from all across the United States and in a myriad of countries outside the states have read my book, viewed my DVDs, and follow my journal articles. I am truly humbled by this response. However, the most gratifying part of this entire experience, without question, is the daily reports I hear from other Blue Collar Investors, many of whom are now my friends, informing me of how my story and system has helped them take control of their financial lives. These are the folks I speak to, and for which my system is designed-average, everyday, hard-working people like me and you, who are smart enough and motivated enough to become CEO of their own money.

So why did I write a second book? Since the penning of my first book, I have received a tremendous amount of email, each and every one of which I have read and deeply appreciate. Thanks to many of you, I now have a huge collection of testimonials, several of which are referenced in this book. I also have received numerous requests for additional information and valuable, constructive criticism, specifically in connection with the topic of Exit Strategies, which was covered in Chapter 11 of *Cashing in on Covered Calls*. Simply put, many have asked for additional information and more examples regarding this topic. After reading this chapter over several times, it appeared writing another book, specifically dedicated to this critical aspect of covered call writing, would be a prudent thing to do. My initial contentions were only confirmed when I ran a search on Amazon.com to discern the amount, if any, of published books focusing on this particular topic. According to Amazon.com, my first book, which kept showing as the #1 "hit" in connection with the foregoing search, was apparently the foremost on the subject of exit strategies for covered call writing. Clearly it was time to write another book focusing on exit strategies.

One more brief point before we get started. My ideas and rules are based not only on common sense, but also on a solid foundation of financial and technical principals. I have read other approaches to exit strategies, agreeing with some and disagreeing with others. This book outlines *my* system for exit strategies, which integrates my love and knack for mathematics along with the aforementioned fundamental and technical principals. While I recognize that there are other ways to handle this particular aspect of covered call writing, for me, my system works best. It is designed to be straightforward and effective. Read it, evaluate it, and then make your own Blue Collar determinations. If this book in some small way is an asset to your investment future, then I have accomplished my mission.

As noted, I will continue to tell you my story, the conclusions I have drawn in the past and those that I intend to use in the future, in the hopes that your mistakes will be few and far between as you take charge of your hard-earned money. I have the utmost confidence that once you've become educated and develop both the confidence and tools to invest on your own, you will no longer need me as a mentor; we'll simply be friends and fellow Blue Collar Investors. As always, I welcome your thoughts and comments about my system and this book in general. After all, if it wasn't for your feedback, it never would have been written.

My very best to all my fellow Blue Collar Investors,
Alan

Acknowledgments

This book could never have been composed without the combined efforts of a team of friends, colleagues, and relatives. I am truly indebted to their selfless efforts that resulted in this publication. First I would like to recognize my wife, Linda; my sons, Jared and Craig; my mother Minnie; and my stepson David Kaplan, whose unending support continues to be a source of motivation and energy. For their care, concern, and management of the written word my thanks goes out to Craig Ellman and Jamie Ellman.

I would also like to single out Barry Bergman, Tony and Ann Marie Covino, and Owen Sargent for their feedback and expertise that greatly enhanced the quality of the completed manuscript.

For her unselfish and generous assistance and guidance I would like to express my gratitude to Barbara Karnes whose friendship I value dearly.

To my brother-in-law, Glenn Shapiro, who worked his magic with the images in this book, I would also like to express my thanks.

My sincere thanks to one and all.

Introduction

I am using this section to get philosophical about stock and option investing in general, and exit strategies in particular. Understanding this logic (I hope you agree with this term) is important. Boring perhaps; but nonetheless important. I'll try to spice it up with a baseball analogy.

For most investors who are learning a strategy there is a range of expectations. If I were to hypothesize the order of preference they would have in following a particular strategy, here is my best guess:

1. Just tell me what to do, and I'll do it (Your beeper goes off and you are told to sell a stock).

2. Give me a system where I will be alerted what to do and when to do it (You set a stop loss order at a certain price point and your broker will sell a stock).

3. Give me a cookbook approach to follow that will lead me to the *only* possible decision (Bank A offers a 4% CD; Bank B offers a 5% CD; I should go to Bank B).

4. I will educate myself and master all aspects of this strategy so that I will be able to come to an intelligent, non-emotional decision in a majority of the situations.

The reason that the first three choices are so popular is that they require little time and effort. The bad news is that they do not work. If they did, we'd all be wearing beepers waiting for that call to action. These are old school approaches to investing and appealing to many due to the lack of education most of us were victims of in the past. We must, therefore, turn to the fourth approach utilizing both education and common sense. This is the philosophy of the Blue Collar Investor System.

Here is my baseball analogy: You are the manager making the calls. It's the ninth inning and your team is behind by one run. If you win the game you're headed for the World Series and a big financial payoff. There's a runner on first and none outs. Are you going to bunt? Hit and run? Swing away? Pinch hit? Steal a base? You have your beeper on but it's not ringing to tell you what to do! Is there only one obvious solution? You start assessing the parameters of the situation. Is the pitcher's windup slow to the plate? How fast is the base runner? Who's on deck? Who's warming up in the bullpen? Who's available on my bench? Can my pitching staff hold the other team to no runs in the next inning? Where are the defenders positioned in the field? So many factors to consider and that darn beeper is still silent. Fortunately, you have mastered all the parameters and have the ability to collate all the information and make an informed decision. You have practiced and experienced similar scenarios and are confident that you are making a proper decision that will give you the best chance to succeed. Is that success guaranteed? NO. But you know that by using your intellect and common sense you have made a better decision than any beeper service, newsletter, media outlet, or any other outside source could ever have produced for you.

You have become an artist. Each stroke on your canvas, by itself, is meaningless. But when you put them all together, you have created a masterpiece. Throw away that beeper, create the next Picasso, and it's off to the World Series!

One

The Basics of Covered Call Exit Strategies—Definitions

This book is written for those who have a solid understanding of the strategy of selling covered call options. In particular, it will address the system set forth in my first book, *Cashing in on Covered Calls*. Since I sell predominantly 1-month options, these exit strategies will address a 4-week or 20-day trading period. **Some contract periods will last 5 weeks or 25 trading days.** However, even if you are a longer term investor, many of the principles of my strategy will still have application just as a fundamental understanding of a particular mathematical formula can be applied to a variety of different situations. Take, for example, the Pythagorean Theorem of right triangles:

$$a(squared) + b(squared) = c(squared)$$

Our grade school teachers asked us to understand the principle of the formula and apply it to find the length of one side of a triangle when given the lengths for the other two. Sometimes we would be asked to use this formula in word problems to find out, for example, the shortest route home. In a similar fashion, we must first understand the basic principles of exit strategies and then apply them to specific, ever-changing sets of circumstances. Most non-Blue Collar Investors (I just made that term up) prefer to simply ask someone what to do, or more commonly, do it for them. How many of you have children who have begged: "Please, please, please do it for me this one time and I'll NEVER ask again?" We, as parents, know that the most prudent and helpful approach is to teach the child how to do it, so it can be duplicated over and over in different situations. That is being a responsible parent. As the saying goes, "Give a man a fish; you have fed him for one day. Teach a man to fish; and you have fed him for a lifetime." While many of you have undoubtedly heard this saying before, it bears repeating, as it highlights one of the core principles of the Blue Collar Investor exit strategy.

While I don't profess to have a definite answer for every situation, I do have a clear understanding of the basic principles of exit strategies that have been working quite well for me these past 10 years. These precepts will have application in most of the situations you will encounter.

Definitions

I will start by reviewing the key terminology used in relation to covered call exit strategies. Most of these terms have been taken from my first book. It is important to learn and master them before moving on.

1. *Exit Strategy* – A plan in which a trader intends to get out of an investment position made in the past. It is a way of cashing out or closing a position. Unless your plan is to do nothing (allow the option to expire or allow assignment of your shares), **all exit strategies begin with buying back the option.**

2. *Assignment* – The receipt of an exercise notice by the option seller (that's us) that obligates us to sell our shares to the option buyer at the specified strike price. Since we are selling *American Style Options,* assignment can take place at any time from the sale of the call option through expiration Friday.

3. *Expiration Friday* – The last day on which an option may be ex-

ercised. This date is the third Friday of the expiration month. If the third Friday of the month is an exchange-recognized holiday, the last trading day is the Thursday immediately preceding this holiday.

4. *Rolling Down* – Closing out an options position at one strike price and simultaneously opening another at a lower strike price in the same contract month.

5. *Rolling Out or Forward* – Closing out an option contract at a near-term expiration date and opening a same strike contract at a later date.

6. *Rolling Up* – Closing out an option contract at a lower strike price and simultaneously opening another at a higher strike price in the same contract month.

7. *Online Discount Broker* – An online stockbroker who carries out *buy and sell orders* at a reduced fee but offers no investment advice.

8. *ESOC* – Ellman System Option Calculator which is an excel calculator used to compute option returns specifically for Alan Ellman's *Cashing in on Covered Calls* system. For exit strategies, the 4th or "What Now" tab will be particularly useful in calculating Expiration Friday exit strategy returns.

9. *Buy to Close* – A term used by many brokerages to represent the closing of a short position (the option sale) in option transactions (buying back the original call option that was sold).

10. *American Style Option* – An option contract that may be exercised at any time between the date of purchase and the expiration date.

11. *Convert Dead Money to Cash Profits* – An exit strategy wherein an option is bought back and the underlying equity sold. The cash

is then used to buy a better performing stock which is used to sell another covered call.

12. *Hit a Double* – An exit strategy wherein an option is bought back and then resold at a higher premium in the same contract period.

13. *Hit a Triple* – An exit strategy wherein an option is bought back twice and resold twice in the same contract period.

These are the definitions you need to know and master for covered call exit strategies. **For a complete list of all definitions used in the** *Cashing in on Covered Calls Strategy,* **see the glossary in the back of this book.** Next, let's explore why it is so critical to employ exit strategies in our investment decisions.

TWO

Why Use Exit Strategies?

One of the most appealing factors that attracted me to investing in covered call options is the control the investor has in the outcome of his or her transaction. As a seller of covered call options, we assume two positions. First, we assume a long position by owning the underlying equity. Second, we incur an obligation by selling the call option; if the option buyer decides to exercise that option, we have the obligation to sell our shares to the buyer at the agreed upon strike price at or prior to the expiration date.

In my system, we have gone to extreme lengths to screen our stocks so that we will only own the greatest performing stocks in the greatest performing industries. That process will dramatically throw the odds in our favor of these securities behaving like good financial soldiers, but does NOT GUARANTEE the same. We must plan for a stock declining in value during the 1-month contract period or for a stock that has increased in value more than the strike price by expiration Friday. In our system of selling covered calls, we can respond to these situations by buying back the option and then taking further appropriate action. Those who do not use exit strategies when selling covered call options are missing out on additional cash profits that can easily be generated simply by adequate education and preparation.

Here are some reasons why we should all be utilizing exit strategies:

1. *Decrease our losses or even increase our profits when the underlying equity declines in value.* We may begin to see a technical breakdown of a stock and become concerned that it could start dropping precipitously. As long as the call option is in an open position, we are required to own those shares. By closing our option position, by buying back the option (buy to close), we are now free to sell the stock or generate additional income by selling another option.

2. *Get out of your stock/option position when new information becomes available.* You may hear news that concerns you but hasn't as yet affected equity value. For example, suppose you hear a report that the CEO of a company whose stock you own is being investigated for possible back-dating of stock options. He denies the allegations and a hearing is set. The stock price is holding but could take a major hit when more news comes out. We, as Blue Collar Investors, stress risk aversion and therefore may want to close our position, sell the stock and get into a safer investment. Another example that I have personally encountered, occurs when a company announces that it will holding a major press release in a few days. This could be great news or distressing news. Once again, why take the chance. Get out now and don't look back. If the news drives the stock way up in price, have no regrets. You did the appropriate thing. This type of conservative approach will pay tremendous dividends in the long run.

3. *Prevent assignment when the current price of the stock is above the strike price.* This normally applies to expiration Friday. When your equity is trading above the strike price (by more than a few cents), assignment will most definitely occur unless you stop it from materializing. If at this time you decide that you still want to own that particular equity, there are times you can

avoid assignment by instituting an expiration Friday exit strategy. Be aware that there are also times when assignment cannot be avoided. Since we are selling American Style Options, the buyer of the option can exercise his right to purchase our shares AT ANY TIME from the sale of the option to expiration Friday. Normally, assignment will occur only after the expiration date, but it infrequently will take place earlier in the contract period. An example of early assignment could be for the option holder to exercise the option in order to capture a dividend distribution. Since there is no way of predicting when or if this will occur here is what I suggest you do if there is early assignment: Say the words *Big Deal* and start immediately planning what you will do with the newly acquired cash in your account to start generating additional profits into your portfolio. Really, it's no big deal!

4. *It will help elevate us into the elite 5-10% of all stock investors.* At this point we are already at an advantage. First, we must remember that 80-90% of all options expire worthless. Is it not to our advantage to be the sellers of a decaying asset rather then the buyers? Furthermore, we have screened our stocks both fundamentally and technically. Then we utilized technical analysis for our buy/sell decisions. We have carefully calculated option returns using the ESOC. If that's not enough, we have factored in more esoteric factors such as earnings reports and monthly same-store retail sales into our investment decisions. Now, by adding in carefully planned out exit strategies, we are elevating ourselves into the top tier of options sellers. This is precisely where Blue Collar Investors belong! I hope at this point you are comfortable with *why* to use exit strategies. We now need to fill in the blanks as to *when* to institute an exit strategy and *which* ones to utilize.

Three

The Mathematics of the 1-Month
Contract Period

Throughout this book, I will reference the 4-week or 20-day contract period. I will stress how I am willing to buy back an option at a higher premium during the earlier, rather than the later portion, of this term. The reason for this is related to the severe degree of time value erosion of the option premiums that occurs during the last 2 weeks of the contract cycle. In addition, there is a greater opportunity to generate profit using an exit strategy if there is more time remaining until expiration Friday.

As noted earlier, all option contracts expire on the 3rd Friday of the month. Most of the time there is one more Friday before the month's end. That means in most instances, a 1-month option contract will last 4 weeks or 20 trading days (less any holidays when the market is closed).

There are, however, a few months where the contract period lasts 5 weeks or 25 trading days (less the days when the market is closed for holidays). This takes place when there are two Fridays remaining in the previous month after expiration Friday. These 5-week contract periods will generate higher option returns due to the increased time value of the premiums.

Here is a monthly breakdown (figure 1) of the contract periods for the calendar year 2008:

Contract Expiration Month	# Weeks in the Contract Period
January	4
February	4
March	5
April	4
May	4
June	5
July	4
August	4
September	5
October	4
November	5
December	4

Figure 1

Since there are 5 trading days per week and 52 weeks per year, there are 260 trading days (less any holidays) in a calendar year. This averages out to approximately 22 trading days per monthly contract period.

Since most contract periods consist of 4 weeks and 20 trading days, I will be using this term as our standard. If we are dealing with the longer of the contract periods, see figure 2 below to interpret the parameters correctly:

4-Week Cycle		5-Week Cycle
Weeks 1 and 2	=	Weeks 1, 2, and 3
Week 3	=	Week 4
Week 4	=	Week 5

Figure 2

For example, if we are willing to buy back an option for 20% or less of the original option sale during weeks 1 and 2 of a 4-week cycle; we are willing to buy it back for the same premium during weeks 1, 2, and 3 of a 5-week cycle. In the next chapter, we will explore the key parameters that will guide us in our exit strategy determinations.

Four

Key Parameters to Consider
Before Expiration Friday

When I first started studying exit strategies in connection with covered call writing, it seemed to be a daunting task that would take endless hours of self-education to master. Unfortunately, it was! Looking back, I now realize what seemed like a complicated strategy at the time, in reality, required only the application of simple common sense and a lot less time to comprehend. An analogy to the movie *Indiana Jones* is instructive. Specifically, in this movie there was a scene in which the villain had Indy trapped; Indy had nowhere to run. To intimidate Indy, the villain pulled out two huge swords and started swirling them about in anticipation of a gruesome beheading. The audience was at the edge of their seats wondering how Indy could possibly escape seemingly imminent disaster. Is there a secret door for him to escape? Are his friends nearby to come to the rescue? It seemed hopeless. But lo and behold, there was a simple common sense, solution. Indy reached into his belt, pulled out a gun, and shot the villain dead right where he stood. Indy proceeded to walk away annoyed at the minor disturbance. In much the same way, figuring out the *when* and *which* of exit strategy decisions is mostly a matter of common sense. To demonstrate, review the following questions and ask yourself if any seem too complicated for comprehension:

1. If there is more time left for an investment to appreciate, do we not have more opportunity to make money?

2. If there is very little time remaining for an investment to appreciate would it not be prudent to avoid spending a lot of money on that particular transaction?

3. If the general stock market is going up, is there not a better chance for the equities within the market to also appreciate?

4. If the market tone is negative, would it not be more difficult for the stocks to appreciate in value?

5. If a stock's technical indicators are mixed is there not a smaller chance of that stock going up in value than if all indicators were positive?

6. If a stock's technicals all turned negative, would we not have a better chance of making money in a different equity with all positive indicators?

7. If we have a calculator that tells us that we can generate great returns from an elite equity, is it not prudent to take advantage of that situation?

8. What is the effect of tannic acid on the gastro-colic reflex? Okay, just kidding about this one.

So there you have it. You get 100% on this common sense test. Now that you have the confidence to proceed, let's examine the key parameters to focus in on for our exit strategy determinations *prior to expiration Friday*. First, let me make one important money-making point:

Use an Online Discount Broker

We will be making a significant number of trades every month. I average between 50-70 contracts each month which doesn't include my stock purchases and sales. It is critical to master this system of investing to the point where you feel 100% comfortable investing without the advice of a professional. Actually, once you become proficient with the methodology, you will probably know more about covered call writing than many brokers. It is essential that we take commissions out of the equation when making our covered call decisions. I call these fees a *non-event*. I currently pay $5.95 per trade up to 1000 shares and under $10 for options contracts. Because the fees are so low, I don't compute them into my calculations or consider them when deciding on instituting exit strategies. I use USAA Brokerage Services. As a former officer in the military, I started using this company and found it to be extremely reliable and inexpensive. You no longer have to be military-related to participate in this brokerage house. Here is the contact information:

www.usaa.com

Here are other brokerages recommended to me by former students (I have no first hand experiences with these companies):
www.thinkorswim.com

www.tdameritrade.com/welcome1.html

www.optionsxpress.com

www.scottrade.com

http://www.tradeking.com/

https://www.schwab.com/

KEY PARAMETERS (prior to expiration Friday)

Time to Expiration and Option Value

Since we are dealing with predominantly 1-month options, there are 4 weeks or 20 days of time value inherent in those option premiums. **Some contract periods will last 5 weeks or 25 trading days**. The decay of time value starts off slowly the first week, begins to increase in the second week, and virtually falls off a cliff during the last 2 weeks.

Here is a diagram (figure 3) that depicts time decay in 1-month option premiums:

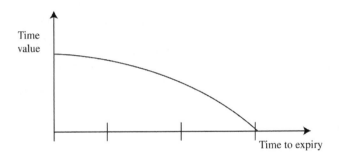

Figure 3

Therefore, there is greater opportunity to make money on an option re-sell earlier in the contract period as opposed to the last 2 weeks. For example, if we sell an option, then buy it back at the end of week 1, we still have 3 weeks remaining for the option value to go back up and sell that very same option. This is the reason that I am willing to pay slightly more to close my option position earlier in the contract period. As time value erodes, it becomes increasingly more difficult to resell another option during the same contract period and make significantly more money than the cost of the *buy-to-close premium*.

This concept of garnering additional income through exit strategies also emphasizes the importance of using an online discount broker to minimize trading commissions. With this common sense approach to the parameter of *time to expiration,* I have developed the following guidelines:

1. **During weeks 1 and 2 (or week 3 as well if we are in a 5-week contract period) of the contract period, buy back the option when the "*ask*" (higher of the bid and ask) is 20% or less of the original option premium.** For example, if we see an option value from our portfolio manager watch list decline to 20 % of the original sale price, we will almost always buy it back. This relieves us of our obligation and sets up the possibility of generating additional cash into our accounts. If we paid $40 per share (investment of $4000 per contract), and sold the call for $1.50 ($150 per contract) that would give us a 3.75% 1-month return. Now, in the event the premium drops to .30, we are left with 20% of the original option premium (.30/1.50)). I am still willing to give up 20% of my original profit because of the possibilities of creating even more profit by selling another call; at worst, my 1-month profit is 3% (80% of the original 3.75%). So as rule #1 above dictates **during the first two weeks of the contract period, buy back the option when its value declines to 20% of the original option premium or less. This will expand to the first 3 weeks in a 5-week contract period.** Now, in another example, if our original option premium was $4 per share or $400 per contract, I would be willing to buy-to-close @ .80 or 20% of the original premium.

2. **During week 3 (week 4 of the 5-week cycle) of the contract period, buy back the option when the "ask" is 10% or less of the original option premium.** Since this is the cycle of the contract period wherein the time value erosion begins to decline precipitously, we are not willing to spend as much as we were during the first two weeks.

3. **During week 4 (week 5 of the 5-week cycle) of the contract period, buy back the option at any price if we feel the <u>neces-</u>**

<u>sity</u> **to sell the underlying equity immediately.** If you still plan to hold onto the underlying stock, there is not enough time left in the contract period to realistically expect to generate an exit strategy profit. However, if the technicals, news or any other factor is cause for concern that the stock price may drop dramatically, buy back the option and sell the stock immediately. More on this situation later in the book.

4. **If <u>at any time</u> during the contract period you have reason to believe that a stock could be in serious danger of dropping dramatically in price, buy back the option <u>at any price</u>, sell the stock, and immediately move the cash into another position**. A case in point would be the examples I referenced in the second of my reasons to utilize exit strategies as follows:

   "Get out of your stock/option position when new information becomes available. You may hear news that concerns you but hasn't as yet affected equity value. For example, suppose you hear a report that the CEO of a company whose stock you own is being investigated for back-dating of stock options. The CEO denies the allegations and a hearing is set. The stock price is holding but could take a major hit when more news comes out. We, as Blue Collar Investors, stress risk aversion and therefore may want to close our position, sell the stock and get into a safer investment. Another example that I have personally encountered, occurs when a company is announces that it will be holding a major press release imminently. This could be great news or distressing news. Once again, why take the chance. Get out now and don't look back. If the news drives the stock way up in price, have no regrets. You did the appropriate thing. This conservative approach will pay tremendous dividends in the long run".

Before I move on to the next parameter to consider, I want to clarify the 20% and 10% calculation figures. If we sell an *at-the-money* or *out-of-the-money strike,* the calculations are easy-we simply take 20%

or 10% of the premium derived from the sale. If, however, we sell an *in-the-money strike*, we must first deduct the *intrinsic value* (the positive difference between the stock price and the strike price) from the option premium to *determine the real return on option (ROO)*. However, *for purposes of evaluating exit strategies, we will consider instituting such a strategy based on 20% or 10% of the entire option premium originally sold, including the in-the-money strikes.* It will simply be easier to compute. More on this subject when we discuss portfolio management lists.

Market Tone

The direction and strength of the general market should play a key role in our investment decisions. When the stock market is declining precipitously, making profits is analogous to riding a bicycle uphill. If, on the other hand, the market is appreciating dramatically, generating great profits is as easy as riding the bicycle downhill. In an up-trending market, we are more likely to base our investment decisions on the likelihood that equities will be driven higher as they get caught up in the momentum of an appreciating equities market. In a market trending downward, our decisions will be based on the greater possibilities of declining stock values. Once again folks, this is not rocket science, simply common sense.

So how do we go about determining market tone? Most of the time information can be gleaned by following the news of the day and watching our portfolios. Picking up a newspaper or turning on our TVs and computers will oftentimes provide the knowledge to make this determination. Many investors prefer the security of a chart to quantify the tone and mood of the market. Two such graphs that would be useful in this regard are those of the S&P 500 and the VIX.

Chart of the S&P 500

The S&P 500 (Standard and Poors 500) is an index consisting of 500 stocks chosen for market size, liquidity and industry grouping, among other factors. It is designed to be a leading indicator of U.S. equities and is intended to reflect the risk/return characteristics of the large-cap universe. Many investors consider this index an accurate reflection of the market in general. See figure 4 [2] as an example of an up trending chart of the S&P 500 that would make us more bullish on our exit strategy decisions:

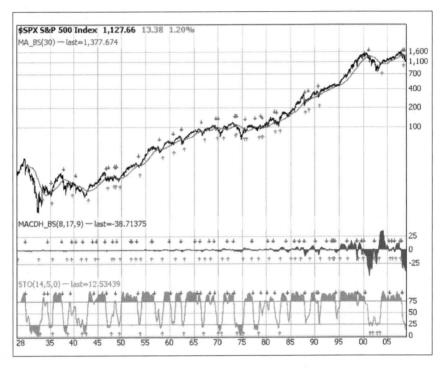

Figure 4

---

2   Investools, www.Investools.com (September, 2006).

On the other hand, Figure 5 [3] represents a chart of the S&P 500 in a severe downtrend, thus representing a bearish outlook for our equities:

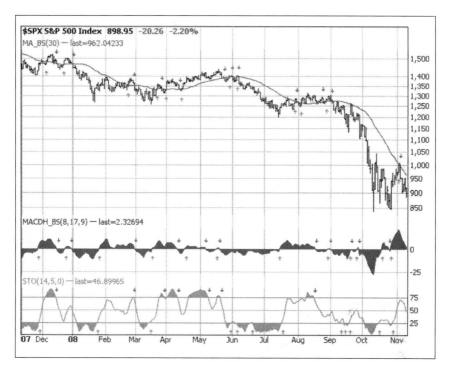

Figure 5

---

3   Investools,www.Investools.com (October, 2008).

Chart of the VIX

The VIX is the ticker symbol for the Chicago Board Options Exchange (CBOE) Volatility Index, which shows the market's expectation of 30-day volatility. It measures market risk and often referred to as the *investor fear gauge*. Values greater than 30 are considered risky due to investor fear, while values under 20 relate to less stressful, calmer times in the market. Therefore, values under 20 can be construed as bullish, where fundamental analysis, as opposed to sheer emotion, should serve as a better indicator. See figure 6 [4] as an example of a chart of the VIX demonstrating an extremely bearish, risky environment for equities:

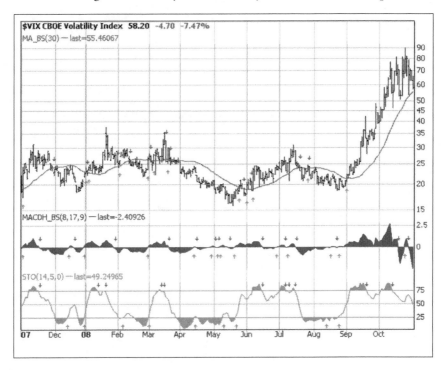

Figure 6

4   Investools, www.Investools.com (October, 2008).

An up trending S&P 500 coupled with a VIX under 20 would represent a bullish sentiment for market tone. If both charts were negative, we have a bearish scenario. If one chart is positive while the other is negative I would consider the situation neutral, and not rely on market tone for my decisions. When creating these charts use the ticker symbols SPX and VIX. A free site for procuring such charts is:

www.stockcharts.com

Technical Analysis of the Underlying Stock

In chapter 8 of my first book, *Cashing in on Covered Calls*, I go into great detail as to how to evaluate a stock from a technical prospective. This is one way, not the only way, to perform such an investigation. The parameters I use are Moving Averages, MACD Histogram, Stochastics and Volume. It is beyond the scope of this book, to redefine these indicators, so please review the information in my first book if you have not yet mastered technical evaluation. I would, however, like to show you a chart of a bullish stock based on all confirming indicators. Figure 7 [5] is a chart of Medco Health Solutions, Inc. (NYSE:MHS) that demonstrates an up trending moving average, with the 20-d ema above the 100-d ema. MACD Histogram is positive and the Stochastic Oscillator has been up trending as well. All these positive indicators occurred on impressive volume:

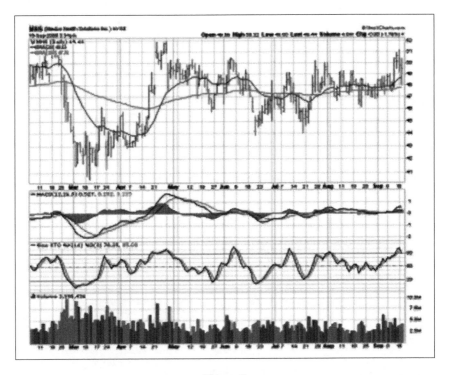

Figure 7

---

5   StockCharts.com (www.stockcharts.com, September, 2008).

When making our exit strategy decisions, a chart with all confirming indicators would be extremely bullish. A mixed technical pattern would be neutral in which case I would tend to be more conservative. If all indicators had turned negative from the initial purchase of the stock and subsequent sale of the option, I would buy back the option and sell the stock immediately.

Calculations

As we journey through the process of preparing for and executing our exit strategies, let's not lose sight of the fact the main reason we are mastering exit strategies is to make money or minimize our losses. As we evaluate time to expiration, cost to *buy to close,* market tone and technical analysis we are formulating the first part of our plan. The second part encompasses computing our returns or potential returns. Chapter 6 of this book will explore exit strategy opportunities where we will utilize the four parameters discussed in this chapter to guide us to our ultimate preference. Although the calculations are important, I use this final parameter as the least significant of the four. If the other factors are describing a stock that will probably continue to depreciate in value, I will opt for an exit strategy that factors that into consideration, even if it is at the expense of a potential higher return. We will go into detail with calculations in the ensuing chapters where examples are given for ALL possible scenarios. The Ellman System Options Calculator (ESOC) will be particularly helpful when calculating Expiration Friday Strategies (see information on the *What Now tab* of the ESOC in Chapter 13). Figure 8 below shows the information gleaned from the *Multiple T*ab of the calculator when computing option returns.

RETURN ON OPTION (ROO) CALCULATOR - MULTIPLE STOCKS

Stock Name or Symbol	Stock $/sh	Option $/sh	Strike $	Expires	Intrisic	Upside	ROO	Up Potential	Down Protect
hcbk (khq-kw)	$ 17.34	$ 1.00	$ 17.50	11/21/08	$ -	$ 0.16	5.8%	0.9%	0.0%
gild (gdq-kv)	$43.03	$ 2.70	$ 42.50	11/21/08	$ 0.53	$ -	5.1%	0.0%	1.2%
gild (gdq-ki)	$ 43.03	$ 1.60	$ 45.00	11/21/08	$ -	$ 1.97	3.7%	4.6%	0.0%
gis (gis-km)	$ 64.73	$ 3.00	$ 65.00	11/21/08	$ -	$ 0.27	4.6%	0.4%	0.0%
chtt (hqt-kn)	$ 67.35	$ 3.50	$ 70.00	11/21/08	$ -	$ 2.65	5.2%	3.9%	0.0%
nke (nke-kk)	$ 57.48	$ 5.20	$ 55.00	11/21/08	$ 2.48	$ -	4.9%	0.0%	4.3%
nke (nke-kl)	$ 57.48	$ 2.60	$ 60.00	11/21/08	$ -	$ 2.52	4.5%	4.4%	0.0%

Designed by: Owen Sargent, CPA (osargentcpa@aol.com)   Run: 11/11/2008 7:27 PM

Figure 8

In formulating our exit strategy, use these four parameters to guide us to the appropriate selection of a specific exit strategy. Before we buy back the option to initiate our course of action, the entire plan should already be thought out. We don't buy back the option and then say to ourselves: "*And now what?*" We have already made that determination.

To this point, we have learned to recognize whether a pre-expiration Friday exit strategy is appropriate using the parameters set forth in this chapter. In the next chapter we will explore the key parameters to evaluate ON or NEAR Expiration Friday.

Five

Key Parameters to Consider on
or near Expiration Friday

Of the four parameters we considered for pre-expiration Friday exit strategies, the first, *time to expiration and option value* is no longer a consideration as there is NO TIME VALUE to speak of on expiration Friday. Nor are we considering the current option value as an entity in and of itself as a factor because on expiration Friday, we will be willing to buy back an option AT ANY PRICE if the concurrent re-sale of the next month's option makes that deal a sensible one. In other words, if the *package* of the cost of the buyback and the subsequent sale of the next month's option yields a respectable return for an equity we are still interested in retaining, then we have an investment we will move forward with. Therefore, the *calculation parameter* becomes much more critical on expiration Friday than during the earlier weeks of the contract period. We are also adding in one additional parameter to consider, *earnings reports*. That being said, here is my list of key parameters to consider when evaluating expiration Friday exit strategies:

Market Tone

As we will discuss in the next chapter, there are several exit strategies to choose from. On expiration Friday, one such consideration will be which strike price to select when re-selling the option. A strongly positive or sometimes a mixed market tone (with concurrent positive stock technicals) will encourage a higher strike price so as to capture both the return on the option premium (ROO) and upside appreciation. A mixed (with concurrent mixed stock technicals) or negative market tone may direct us to the lower of the strike prices.

Technical Analysis of the Underlying Stock

This parameter is important for two reasons. First, before employing an expiration Friday exit strategy, we are required to make sure that the equity is still fundamentally and technically sound. This is part of our original system requirement to only own the greatest performing stocks. If the security is sound technically, with either all confirming indicators positive or moving average positive and one or more confirming ones negative or neutral, that stock is eligible for an exit strategy maneuver. The second reason this parameter is important relates to the strike price. As with market tone, we are more likely to re-sell at the higher strike price if the technicals are all positive, rather than mixed. If the technicals are all negative, we are required to sell the stock. This is an unlikely scenario since the market price has exceeded the strike price (the only time we consider an expiration Friday exit strategy), so the chart pattern should still be quite healthy. If we do decide that the stock needs to be sold, *no action needs to be taken on our part.* Share assignment will occur over the weekend, after 4PM, on expiration Friday, and the cash from that sale will be in our account by the following Monday.

Earnings Reports

In chapter 12 of *Cashing in on Covered Calls,* I give detailed reasons why it is critical to avoid earnings reports when selling covered call options. As we approach expiration Friday we need to check our portfolio manager list or ER Website (www.earningswhispers.com) to make certain that this equity will not be reporting in the upcoming contract period. If the equity will be reporting in the upcoming contract period we have three choices:

1. Allow assignment and use the cash to purchase a different equity the following week.

2. Buy back the option and own the stock through the earnings report without selling an option. This way, if the ER is positive, we can get the full appreciation of the stock without being limited by a strike price. This second choice is NOT part of my system of selling covered call options. I mention it because I am asked about this scenario at each and every one of my seminars. If you are sticking strictly to a covered call strategy, allow share assignment if the ER is going to be announced the upcoming contract period.

3. If the ER is reported early in the next contract period, allow the shares to be sold, and buy them back a day or two after the report assuming all system criteria are still in place. At this point you are again free to again start cashing in on covered calls with that same equity.

Calculations

Let us review the list of circumstances that need to materialize in order to be in a position to calculate potential expiration Friday option returns:

1. The current market value of our stock is greater than the agreed upon strike price.

2. The fundamentals and technicals of the equity still meet our system criteria.

3. We have evaluated market tone and stock technicals to help guide us to an appropriate strike price determination. The more

positive these indicators are, the more likely we are to roll out and up as opposed to rolling out only.

4. There is no earnings report scheduled for the upcoming contract period.

If all four of these criteria are met, then we will do our calculations to determine if that stock will be in or out for the next contract period. We use the *What Now* tab of the calculator to determine our returns and compare those to the ones we would get from selling the stock and utilizing a different financial soldier. The next two chapters will discuss the exit strategy alternatives and calculations available to us prior to expiration Friday and on or near expiration Friday. After completion of these two chapters, I will provide a series of examples that will cover all the possible scenarios (that I can think of....cut me some slack on that one!).

Six

Exit Strategy Alternatives
Prior to Expiration Friday

This chapter will discuss four possible exit strategies; Rolling down (a common options term), taking no immediate action after buying back the option thereby creating an opportunity to *hit a double* (my term), *converting dead money to cash profits* (another blue collar term) and taking no action whatsoever. All apply in situations where the underlying stock has declined in price causing the associated option premium to depreciate as well. Our rules for option buy-backs during weeks 1 and 2 are to spend no more than 20% of the original option sale; no more than 10% during week 3, and at any price if it is critical to sell the stock. Refer to figure 2, page 13 to see the corresponding weeks in a 5-week cycle.

1. Rolling Down

Rolling down occurs when we buy back a previously sold option (buy to close our position) and simultaneously sell another option at a lower strike price. Let's assume we buy 100 shares of company XYZ @ $38 per share. We then sell the $40 call @$2. This represents a 1-month 5% return. One week later the price drops to $35 per share and the corresponding option value also declines to .40. This *does* meet our requirement of no more than 20% of the original option premium ($2 x .20 = .40). At the same time, the $35 strike is selling for $2. This is a defensive play as we are garnering an additional $160 per contract ($200 - $40 = $160 for the 100 shares). This will also result in a probable loss of $3 per share or $300 per contract on the share depreciation (purchased for $38 per share and required to sell for $35 per share). If the value of the stock is below $35 at expiration Friday, the shares will not be assigned and sold. Assuming, however, that the shares are sold, here's how to calculate the result:

Income from two option sales: $200 (original option sale) + $160 (second sale minus the cost of the buyback) = $360 profit.

Loss from stock depreciation: $3800 (100 shares @$38) - $3500 (sold @ $35/share) = $300.

Our net gain is $360 - $300 = $60 profit

Therefore, by instituting a rolling down exit strategy, we generated a $60 profit despite the fact that our asset (stock) depreciated in value by $300.

We lean towards a rolling down strategy when the market tone and technicals are mixed to negative. I would also be more inclined to use this strategy later rather than earlier in the contract period (late in week 2 and week 3, rather than week 1).

2. Take No Immediate Action – Create an Opportunity to Hit a Double

Can you tell that I'm a baseball fan? It's my book, so I can call it whatever I want! In this scenario, we buy back the option as long as it meets our 20%/10% requirements. Once we execute this trade (buy to close), we simply watch the stock price and take no immediate action. Our goal is that the underlying equity will appreciate in value in a relatively short period of time, thereby driving up the option value. If this occurs, we can sell the exact same option (strike and month) and generate a second profit from the same option, or, in other words, *hit a double*. (I once hit a triple but I don't want to dwell on it as it may sound like I'm bragging.) For example, we sell an option for $2, buy it back one week later for .40, and resell it for $1 the next week. This will generate an additional $60 per contract into our account with only a few clicks of our computer.

If the stock does not appreciate in value, we can then look to rolling down or our third possible strategy, selling the stock. By the way, did I mention that I once hit a triple?

We utilize this strategy when the market tone and stock technicals are mixed to positive and earlier in the contract period (especially during the first week or early in the second).

3. Convert Dead Money to Cash Profits

This strategy should be considered when there is a dark cloud hanging over our stock. We worked so hard to properly identify one of the greatest performing stocks in a strong industry but assume, for whatever reason, this equity is not behaving. It will happen. You may have even allowed this stock to remain in your portfolio an additional contract period (perhaps against your better judgment). The price has dropped, the technicals are deteriorating and you are losing patience with this financial soldier. Now take note and underline the next sentence (never mind, I'll underline it for you): <u>There is nothing wrong with selling a stock that is not performing.</u> This is one of the most difficult concepts for investors to accept. Many assume that if they sell, they are losing money and if they don't, there is no loss.

Here is my common sense (I hope you concur) approach to this situation: the cash in that stock is what is important; the stock itself is merely a vehicle that is temporarily bringing that cash out into the investment battlefield in hopes of coming home with friend$ (no misprint). If that equity is not producing, it needs to be replaced with a stronger warrior. This point can be demonstrated by asking yourself the following question: "at this point in time, is that cash more likely to generate profit in a stock with poor technicals and declining market value, or by purchasing a different stock with great technicals and an up trending share price?" Granted, the laggard stock may turn around and head back up. The new stock we buy may change direction as well.

There are no guarantees. However, we **are** throwing the odds in our favor by using sound fundamental and technical principles, in addition to a whole lot of common sense.

Since the stock has been depreciating in price, so has the option value. We buy back the option at any price, sell the poor-performer, purchase a new stock and proceed to sell the option on that healthier gladiator. We make every effort to generate a profit on this exchange, and most of the time, we will. Keep in mind, however, that the main purpose behind this maneuver is to avoid a major loss on the value of the underlying equity.

We utilize this strategy when the stock technicals are negative and the stock price has dropped with little sign of near-term improvement. This choice can be utilized at any time during the contract period prior to expiration Friday.

4. No Action Taken

As free-thinking Blue Collar Investors, taking no action should always be considered. Assume there is no clear cut choice from the three mentioned above. Perhaps the calculations don't impress you, or maybe you just want to see how things turn out by the end of the contract period; after all, we are only talking about a 1-month obligation. The *No Action Taken* is a choice I tend to favor in the latter part of the contract period when the possibilities of creating exit strategy profits have declined. As long as you have appropriately evaluated the other choices and don't feel excited about them, feel free to take no action. It could turn out to be the best decision.

So there you have it…the exit strategy possibilities for weeks 1 through 4 prior to expiration Friday. Please remember that **some contract periods will last up to 5 weeks, or 25 trading days.** In these cases weeks 1, 2 and 3 will be one category, week 4 replaces the old week 3 and week 5 becomes the final week. Until you have these concepts mastered, I thought that it would be useful to create a *Situation Form* (see figure 9) to help evaluate various circumstances and the corresponding possible exit strategies best utilized with each, given the aforementioned parameters. After entering the name of the stock, circle <u>one</u> choice in each of the next 4 rows. Then enter <u>as many exit strategy possibilities</u> available to you in this situation .Use the *Analysis Area* for notes and comments to help guide you to these decisions. After doing this exercise a few dozen times, you will be able to manage your conclusions without the form as it becomes second nature to you. I will use the format of this form in examples I give in the later chapters of this book.

*This is the form for the 4-week cycle. Change the weeks according to figure 2, page 13 for a 5-week cycle.

Situation Form- Pre-Expiration Friday

Name of Stock _____

Week of Contract Period	1 or 2	3	4
Current/Original Option $	20% or less	10% or less	More than 20%
Market Tone	Positive	Mixed	Negative
Technical Analysis	Positive	Mixed	Negative
Exit Strategy Choice	Roll Down	Hit a Double	No Action

Convert Dead $ to Cash Profits

Exit Strategy Analysis

Figure 9

See Appendix VII for some exit strategy possibilities.

In the next chapter, we will discuss the choices we have on or near the expiration of our contracts.

Seven

Exit Strategy Alternatives on or near Expiration Friday

Mastering alternative exit strategies on or near expiration Friday will produce tremendous profits for you in the long run. As we approach expiration Friday you will note that certain of your equities are trading at or above the agreed upon strike price. Congratulations for selecting such great stocks! In these instances, you have generated a significant 1-month profit on the sale of the option (ROO) and perhaps on equity appreciation if you sold an out-of-the-money call. Either way, you have done quite well with this investment. Despite the fact that we are selling *American Style Options* that can be exercised at any time from option sale through expiration Friday, share assignment normally will not occur until after the contract expires. For example, if you sold a $50 call and the current market price is $52 on expiration Friday, your shares will be sold over the weekend and this sale along with the additional cash generated in your account will be reflected in your online account on Saturday or Sunday. As CEO of your own money, it is your obligation to determine if it is in your best interest to allow that to happen. You are in control of this situation. During this period, there are three exit strategies choices available to us; rolling out, rolling out and up, and taking no action at all thereby allowing share assignment.

1. Taking No Action

In this case, you decide that it is best to allow your shares to be sold and use the cash generated from that sale to purchase another financial soldier to join your army the next month. Perhaps there is an earnings report coming out in this next contract period. In this scenario, you must sell the stock by allowing assignment or own it up through the earnings report and not sell the corresponding option (not part of my covered call system). Similarly, there may be concerns with the technical indicators that suggest you should sell the stock. Finally, the calculations may lead you to the conclusion that the cash in that particular equity may be better utilized in a different stock that will generate more income.

If this is the path you decide to take, no action is required on your behalf. As long as your shares are above the strike price they will, most likely, be sold after expiration Friday. When you check your online account on Saturday or Sunday, you will see that you no longer own those shares, and that the cash generated from that sale will be available for use on Monday. There will be a commission charged to you (a non-event for online discount brokerages) for this transaction. Your next step is then to plan how to best utilize this cash in the upcoming contract period. The quicker you put that cash to work (after intelligent, non-emotional analysis), the greater your profits will be.

2. Rolling Out (forward)

In this strategy we close out our option contract (buy to close) and immediately sell the <u>next month's same strike contract</u>. To get to this point, we have already determined that the stock fundamentals and technicals are still in place as far as meeting our system criteria. We have also ascertained that there is no upcoming earnings report to interfere with this deal. Finally, the calculations are such that we have come to the conclusion that the cash in this equity will be most productive by holding the stock. In other words, we still love the stock and the returns it generates. Here is a real life example I give on page 123 of *Cashing in on Covered Calls*:

- I owned 100 x AAPL currently trading for $72.47

- Previously sold (1) of the $72.50 call (strike price was the result of a stock split)

- Apple Computer had been appreciating in value and there was a significant chance of share assignment (share price had to go up only a few more cents).

- The stock's fundamentals and technicals were still in place with no upcoming ER.

- Market tone was positive.

- The buyback of the $72.50 call cost $1.80 per share or $180 per contract.

- Reselling the next month's <u>same strike (roll out) </u>of $72.50 would generate a profit of $440 per contract.

- To calculate our return, we subtract $180 from $440 and divide by our cost basis (current market value of the 100 shares):

$440 - $180/ $7247 = 3.6% 1-month return or 44% annualized.

The question we Blue Collar Investors pose to ourselves is: "*is this a good place to put the available cash ($7247) this upcoming contract period?*" I think you would all agree that given the situation and the calculations, it would be difficult to say no.

Rule: When we roll out, we always do so to an *in-the-money strike*. The reason for this relates to the very nature of a rolling out exit strategy on or near expiration Friday. The share value is higher than the strike and we roll out to the next month's same strike. In the previous example, the assumption was that AAPL would surpass the $72.50 strike price by expiration Friday. Therefore, the strike is in-the-money (lower than) as compared to the stock price. Consequently, we are also gaining some downside protection when rolling out as we would if we sold any in-the-money strike. That amount is equal to the intrinsic value of the option premium. To calculate downside protection after rolling out, divide the intrinsic value by the current market value of the shares or the strike price whichever is less. For example, had we rolled out to a $40 strike when the stock value was $42, our downside protection would be as follows:

$$\$42 - \$40/\$40 = 5\%$$

Remember, the *What Now* tab of the ESOC will do all these calculations for you.

We use the rolling out strategy when the current market value is at or more than the previously sold strike price, market tone is mixed to positive, stock technicals are mixed to positive, there is no ER coming out in the upcoming contract period, calculations show a good return and you are uncertain about share appreciation.

3. Rolling Out and Up

When we Roll Out and Up, we close out our option contract (buy to close) and immediately sell the <u>next month's higher strike contract</u>. To get to this point, we have already determined that the stock fundamentals and technicals are still in place as far as meeting our system criteria. We have also ascertained that there is no upcoming earnings report to interfere with this deal. In addition, we also feel that there is an excellent chance that the stock will continue to climb in value. Finally, the calculations are such that we have come to the conclusion that the cash in this equity will be most productive by staying in this same stock. In other words, we still love the stock and the returns it generates. Here is a real life example I give on pages 123 and 124 of *Cashing in on Covered Calls*:

- The same scenario as in the *rolling out example*.

- Stock technicals are very strong and we feel that there is a substantial possibility of continued share appreciation.

- Buy back the $72.50 call for the same $180.

- Sell the next month's $75 call (roll out and up) for $330.

- Calculate our returns:

  $330 - $180 = $150/$7247 = 2.1% = 25% annualized

- If the stock surpasses the $75 strike price by the end of the contract period, we will have earned an additional $253: ($75 - $72.47) x 100 = $253.

- Add $253 to the $150 profit from the option buyback and resale, we get a total potential profit of $403.

- Our return would then be $403/$7247 = 5.6% for 1 month or 67% annualized.

Rule: You can roll out and up to an in-the-money strike OR an out-of-the-money strike. *There are also times when your stock is sitting at the next higher strike, in which case you are rolling out and up to an at-the-money strike (see the APOL example in Chapter 10).

It is important to understand the mathematics of these two situations when deciding between rolling out or rolling out and up. While it is true that the ESOC will do all these calculations for you, understanding how we get to these results will make you better investors. To clarify, the following are explanations for each scenario (for rolling out and up) along with analogies that have worked well in my seminars:

Situation:

- Buy 100 x XYZ @ $78.

- Sell Sept. $80 strike.

- Current Price is $83 on or near expiration Friday.

- Current value of our investment is $8000 (if we allow assignment that is what we will receive).

Rolling Out and Up-Out-Of-The-Money

- Buy back the Sept. $80 @ $3.10.

- Sell the Oct. $85 @ $4.20.

- Profit is $110 (420 – 310) but there is more.

- We have *bought up* the value of our stock from $80 to $83 = $300. Let me explain via the following analogy: Your next door neighbor is 83 inches tall (current price of the stock). You invite him into your kitchen which has an 80 inch high ceiling (current strike price). How tall is your neighbor in your kitchen if you measure him from head to toe (what is the value of your stock with an 80 strike)? The answer to both is 80. Now, you and your neighbor move into your dining room which has an 85 inch ceiling (rolled up to an 85 strike). How tall is your neighbor now, in your dining room (how much is your stock worth with an 85 strike) if you measure him from head to toe? The answer to both is 83. You have increased his height (bought up the value of the stock) from 80 to 83.In other words, the option premium we pay to buy back the option is allowing the equity value to increase from $80 per share to $83 per share. We need to account for such adjustments in our calculations:

- Profit is $110 + $300 = $410/ $8000 = 5.1% 1-month return or 62% annualized.

- We also have upside potential (stock can appreciate from $83 to $85) or $200. The calculation for this is 200/8000 = 2.5%.

- The total possible 1-month profit is: 410 +200/8000 = 7.6% or 91% annualized.

If we only factored in the original $110 profit the results would not look nearly as impressive: 110/8000 = 1.4% compared to the possible 7.6% depicted above.

In the next example we will roll out and up, in-the-money.

Situation:

- Buy 100 x XYZ @ $78.

- Sell Sept. $80 strike.

- Current Price is $86 on or near expiration Friday.

- Current value of our investment is $8000 (if we allow assign-ment that is what we will receive).

Rolling Out and Up- In-The-Money

- Buy back the Sept. $80 @ $6.10

- Sell the Oct. $85 @ $4.20 for a *loss* of $190 per contract, but there's more.

- We have *bought up* the value of our stock from $80 (amount we would receive if we permit assignment) to $85 = $500 per con-tract. Let's go back to our analogy: This time, your neighbor is 86 inches tall (you obviously live in the land of the giants!). This is akin to the current market price of the stock. In your kitchen (80 inch ceiling/strike) your neighbor is 80 inches tall if mea-sured from head to toe. You invite him into your dining room which has the 85 inch ceiling (rolling up to the 85 strike). Now your neighbor has gone from 80 inches tall in your kitchen to 85 inches tall in your dining room. Even though he is 86 inches tall, he only measures 85 from head to toe because of the ceiling (strike price) restriction. We need to add that extra value to our calculations:

- $500 – $190 = $310/ $8000 = 3.9% 1-month return or 47% annualized.

- Since this is an *in-the-money strike*, we also have downside pro-tection equal to the intrinsic value of the option premium. In this case the intrinsic value is $100 (86 – 85 x 100) = 100. Our downside protection is therefore 100/8000 = 1.3 %.

Had we only factored in the initial calculation, we would have seen a net loss of $190 and never considered this possibility. By factoring in the increase in equity value the rolling out and up strategy created, we get a truer picture of the exit strategy benefit. Knowledge is power, a path to great profits and ultimately a path to financial freedom.

We use the rolling out and up strategy when the current market value is at or more than the previously sold strike price, market tone is mixed to positive, stock technicals are positive, there is no ER coming out in the upcoming contract period, calculations show a good return and you are relatively confident about share appreciation. This is a more bullish maneuver than simply rolling out.

So there you have it…the exit strategy possibilities for the time period on or around expiration Friday. Until you have these concepts mastered, I thought it would be useful to create a *Situation Form* (see figure 10 below) to help evaluate various circumstances and the possible exit strategies best utilized, given these parameters. After entering the name of the stock, circle <u>one</u> choice in each of the next 3 rows. Then enter the calculations for rolling out, rolling out and up, both in and out of the money. Use the *Analysis Area* for notes and comments to help guide you to these decisions. After doing this exercise a few dozen times, these concepts will become second nature, and you will able to manage your conclusions without the form. I will use the format of this form in examples I give in the later chapters of this book.

*This is the form for the 4-week cycle. Change the weeks according to figure 2, page 13 for a 5-week cycle.

<u>Situation Form- On or Near Expiration Friday</u>

Name of Stock _____

ER Coming Out? YES_____ NO_____

Market Tone Pos._____Mixed_____ Neg._____

Tech. Analysis Pos._____Mixed_____ Neg_____

Rolling Out Calculation: _____

Rolling Out and Up I-T-M _____

Rolling Out and Up O-T-M _____

Exit Startegy Choice Rolling Out_____Rolling Out and Up I-T-M_____

No Action _____Rolling Out and Up O-T-M_____

<u>EXIT STRATEGY ANALYSIS</u>

Figure 10

See Appendix VIII for a flow chart of some exit strategy possibilities.

Eight

Preparing Your Portfolio Manager Watch List for Exit Strategies

In my first book, *Cashing in on Covered Calls*, I devote chapter 10 to Portfolio Management; the art and science of making decisions about investment mix and policy, matching investments to objectives, asset allocation, and balancing risk versus performance. *It requires organized lists of accurate information.*

One of the lists in our portfolio manager is the catalog of options sold that particular month. When those options expire or the positions closed via exit strategies, that particular option is deleted from the list and the replacement option is added. A typical options watch list is found in figure 11 on the following page:

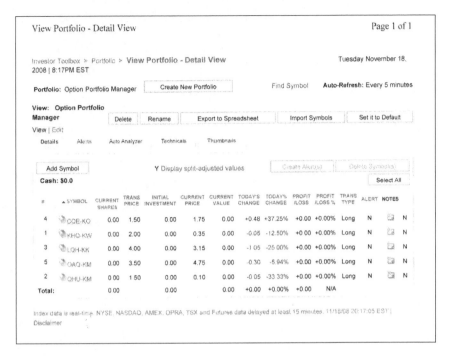

Figure 11

Notice that option ticker KHQ-KW was originally sold for $2.00 per share. This is found under the *transaction price*. Now, according to our system, we will consider buying back the option @ 20% (.40) or 10% (.20) depending on the week of the contract period. In this example, the current option price is .35 therefore it would be eligible for an exit strategy if we were in the first 2 weeks of a 4-week contract period or the first 3 weeks of a 5-week contract period. You may find it easier, when entering the contract information on this list, to enter 20% of the transaction price rather the actual price so as to have a quick and easy comparison as depicted figure 12:

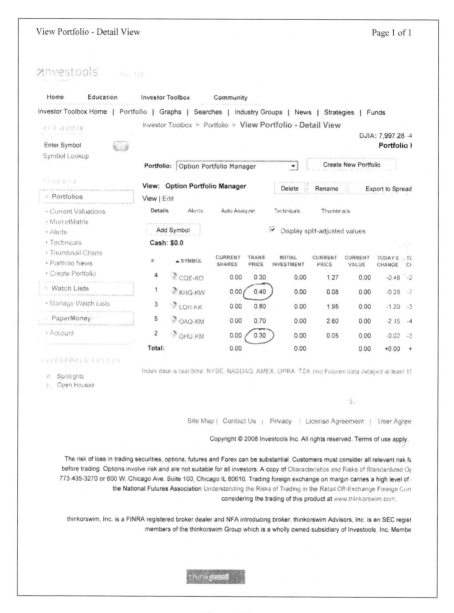

Figure 12

A quick glance of this option (KHQ-KW) shows a current value of .08 which is below our .40 or .20 threshold requirement for an exit strategy. That means it's time to take action. As we approach two weeks remaining in the contract period, the figure of .40 would be cut in half to .20, representing the 10% rule starting in the second from the last week. **Please bear in mind that I am providing you guidelines; once you are comfortable with the system, it's okay to deviate slightly from these guidelines.** In other words, if an option value is sitting at 22% of its original sale price in the first week and you feel that an exit strategy is in your best interest, go for it. In some of the examples that I will be giving you, I may have bought back an option at slightly more than the 20% criterion. However, in the beginning, while you are learning and evaluating the system, try to adhere to the above-noted guidelines as closely as possible. Investing in stock options is as much an art as it is a science. Eventually, I would like to see that *artist* in you flourish as much as possible!

Nine

Executing the Exit Strategy Trades

Executing these exit strategy trades is very similar to the procedures involved in selling covered calls. This execution process can be broken down into simple, straightforward steps. To be as thorough as possible, below is a brief listing of the procedural steps involved in executing exit strategies. To set the stage, assume you previously sold a covered call option and have now decided to invoke an exit strategy. The following list assumes you have done your due-diligence, calculations and have option ticker information at your fingertips:

1. Go to your online brokerage account.

2. Hit the *place trade* link.

3. Under *transactions*, scroll down to *options* and click on that link.

4. Under *actions*, scroll to *buy-to-close*.

5. Scroll to and highlight the *specific option* you are buying back.

6. Enter the # of contracts.

7. Click on *limit order*.

8. Enter the *limit price* which is the *ask* or higher of the bid-ask.

9. Under *duration*, hit *day only*.

10. Now hit *place order*.

11. Check your *order status*.

12. Once *executed*, go back to *trade*.

13. Hit *options*.

14. Hit *sell covered call*.

15. Type in *option symbol*.

16. Enter the *# of contracts*.

17. Hit *limit order*.

18. The *limit price* is the bid or the *lower of the bid-ask*.

19. *Duration* is *day only*.

20. *Place order*.

21. Confirm trade *execution* by checking order status.

CONGRATULATIONS! You have just successfully executed an exit strategy.

Ten

Real Life Examples Prior to Expiration Friday

In both this chapter and 11, real life examples will be given demonstrating the implementation and use of all exit strategies discussed in this book thus far. My objective is to bestow a certain level of comfort with which you can use this information and apply it to every situation you may face in your investment life. Just like learning that math formula and then applying it to a word problem, discussed in Chapter 1, the exit strategies discussed thus far and the core principles underlying each can be applied to formulate decisions in a myriad of different scenarios.

Here is the information and how it will be organized in the proceeding examples:

1. Exit Strategy Invoked

2. Situation Information
   - Week of contract period
   - Market Tone
   - Technical Analysis of Stock

3. One Month price Chart of Stock

4. One Month Price Chart of Option- *I use these to show the association between equity price and option value. Calculations are approximate due to differences in bid-ask prices. The concept, rather than the specific numbers, is of overriding importance.*

5. Calculations, when applicable (commissions will be omitted since we use online discount brokers).

6. Analysis or the thought process behind the decisions.

As you become more familiar with the process of collating the information and coming to a conclusion, you may see other ways of handling these exit strategies. Remember, this is an art as well as a science. When you start to locate other viable opportunities, that's when you know that you are beginning to master the system. Thinking outside the box is something I encourage, respect, and admire.

In this and the next few chapters, I am using charts from the contract period ending on November 21, 2008. This was a 5-week contract period so the 20% rule applies to the first 3 weeks; the 10% rule to the 4th week; and expiration Friday strategies will occur during the 5th week.

In this chapter we will explore examples of exit strategies available *prior to expiration Friday.* Chapter 11 will describe exit strategy opportunities *on or near expiration Friday,* while chapter 12 will highlight stocks with multiple exit strategy utilization within the same contract period. **All stock and option charts and option chains are taken from Investools, Investor Education (www.investools.com).** *Please note that where you see a "$" on a chart, this represents the day the earnings report was made public.*

These 30-d charts are NOT appropriate for technical analysis of stocks but are to be used <u>exclusively</u> to show the relationship between share price and option premium.

Hitting a Double

Situation when hitting a double:

We are in the first three to four weeks of the 5-week contract period; market tone is mixed to positive; and technical analysis of the stock is positive.

Example 1- AFAM

Charts:

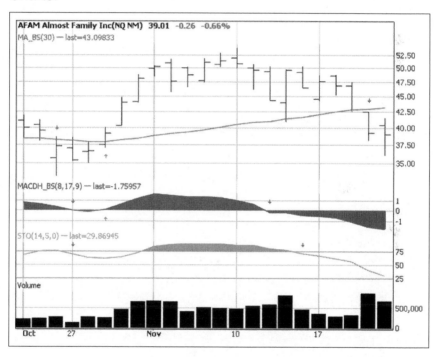

Figure 13

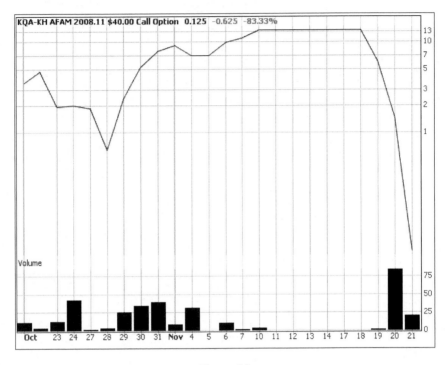

Figure 14

Calculations:

10/20/08- Buy 100 x AFAM @ 40
10/20/08- Sell 1 x Nov. 40 Call @ $3.50 for a 1-month 8.75% return
10/28/08- Buy to close 1 x Nov. 40 Call @ .60 (meets our 20% rule)
10/30/08- Re-sell 1 x Nov. 40 call @ $5.10

This generates an additional $450 into our account ($510 - $60 = $450), which represents an additional 11% 1-month return. Our total return of $800 (350 + 450) represents a total 1-month return of 20% because we invoked an exit strategy wherein we *hit a double*.

Analysis:
This is the ideal situation to hit a double. We have a great performing stock in a great performing industry that gives us a fabulous 1-month option return. By selling this at-the-money call there is no hope of eq-

uity appreciation. However, the stock takes a dip in the first week and we jump on the opportunity to buy back the option and relieve ourselves of the obligation. Since we still like everything about the stock, we wait to see if the stock price goes back up. In this case we have plenty of time. Just two days later, the stock appreciates dramatically as does the call option. This increase can be easily viewed on both charts. Normally I will give the stock at least a week to appreciate but in this scenario we didn't have to wait that long. I re-sold the same exact option two days later for a significant profit. Most of the time when you hit a double the second profit will be less than the first because of time decay. In this particular example, the stock shot up so much and so quickly that the reverse occurred. The return in this case was well above average, however, because the chart patterns where so clear, I felt obliged to include this example. You will see returns of this nature from time to time but not frequently. We'll take it!

Example 2- BLUD

Charts:

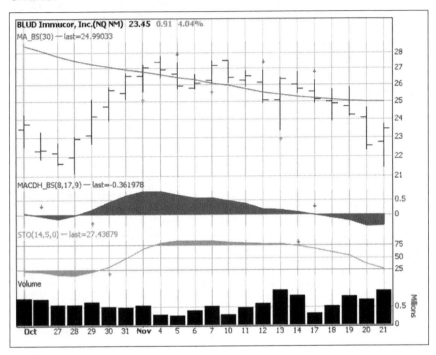

Figure 15

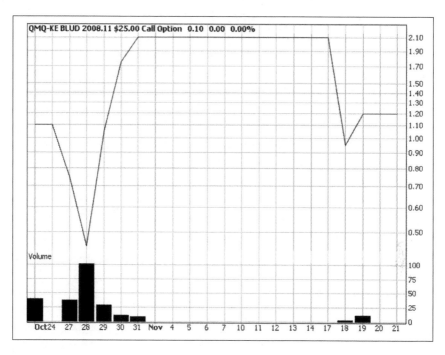

Figure 16

Calculations:

> 10/20/08- Buy 100 x BLUD @ $23.80
> 10/20/08- Sell 1 x $25 Call @ $1.10 for a 1-month return of 4.6%
>   (110/2380)
> 10/28/08- Buy to close 1 x $25 Call @ .20 (meets our 20% rule)
> 10/30/08- Re-sell 1 @ $25 Call @ $1.70

This generates an additional $150 into our account (170 – 20) which represents an additional 6.3% 1-month return. The total 1-month return for this investment is $260 (110 + 150) or 10.9% (110 + 150/2380).

Analysis:

This example is quite similar to the previous one (AFAM) with the returns, although stupendous, not quite as high. Once again, by being aware of exit strategies, we can significantly enhance our profits.

Rolling Down

Situation when rolling down:

We are in the first three to four weeks of the 5-week contract period; market tone is mixed to negative; and technical analysis of the stock is mixed.

Example 1- HAS

Charts:

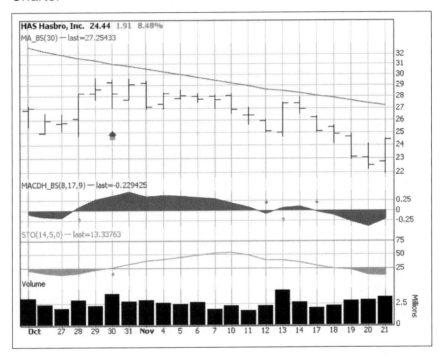

Figure 17

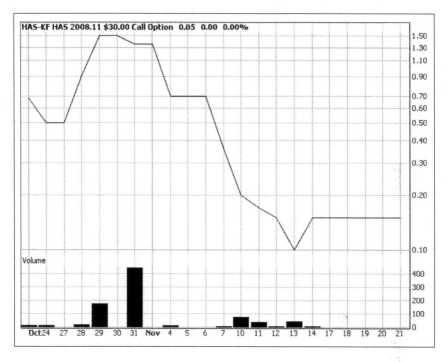

Figure 18

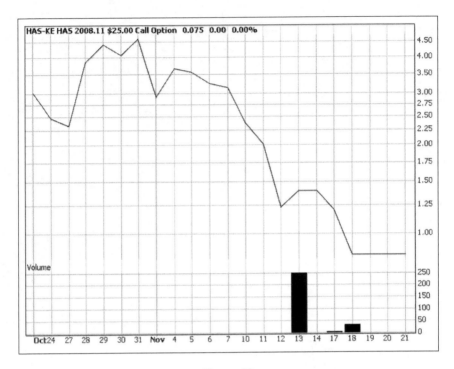

HAS-KE HAS 2008.11 $25.00 Call Option 0.075 0.00 0.00%

Figure 19

Calculations:

> 10/29/08- Buy 100 x HAS @ $28.50
> 10/29/08- Sell 1 x $30 Call @ 1.50
> 11/11/08- Buy to close 1 x 30 Call @ .15 (meets our 10% rule)
> 11/11/08- Sell 1 $25 Call @ $2.00

The rolling down strategy generated an additional $185 per contract (200– 15).

Analysis:

From the time of purchase on the 29th of October, HAS had been deteriorating in price. The total profit generated from the two option sales is $335 (150 + 185). The total loss on the equity depreciation is $350 (2850 – 2500). The net loss on this investment is $15. By utilizing the rolling down strategy we turned a $350 loss into a $15 loss.

Example 2- RS

Charts:

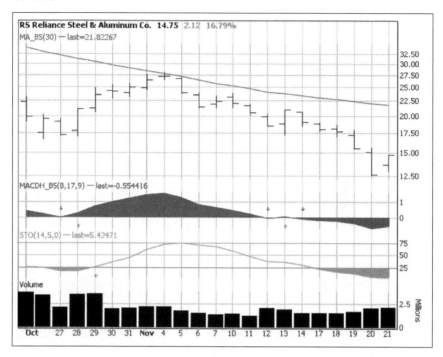

Figure 20

Figure 21

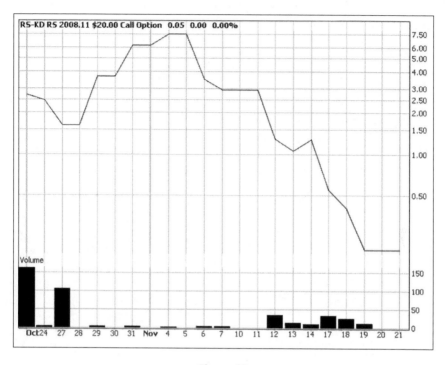

Figure 22

Calculations:

> 10/20/08- Buy 100 x RS @ $20
> 10/20/08- Sell 1 x $22.50 Call @ $1.50
> 11/13/08- Buy to close $22.50 call @ .15 (meets our 10% rule)
> 11/13/08- Sell 1 $20 Call @ $1.10
> 11/21/08- RS closed the contract period @ $15.

This rolling down strategy generates another $95 per contract (110 – 15) into our account.

Analysis:

After appreciating in value the first week, RS declined in value for the remainder of the contract period. The total premium generated this month was $245 (150 + 95). Our total loss on this investment was $255 (500 – 245) since the price declined from $20 to $15. This example demonstrates that, although losses will occur, by utilizing exit strategies, we can minimize those losses, and sometimes break even (as in example 1) or even make a profit.

Example 3- SYNA

Charts:

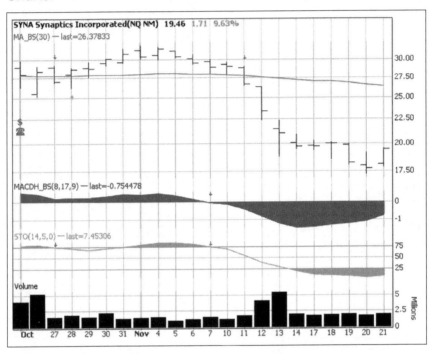

Figure 23

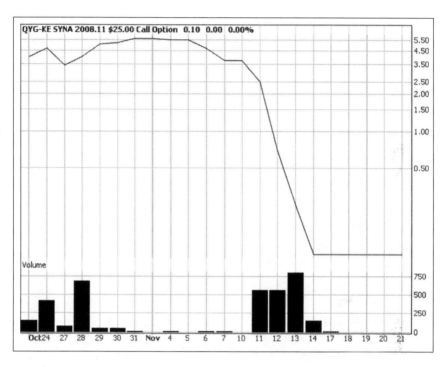

Figure 24

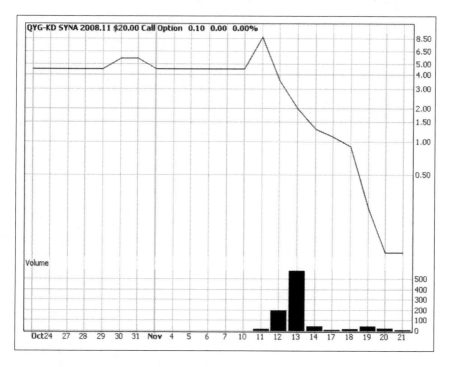

Figure 25

Calculations:

10/21/08- Buy 100 x SYNA @ $27
10/21/08- Sell 1 x $25 Call @ $4.50
11/13/08- Buy to close 1 x $25 Call @ .20 (meets our 10% rule)
11/13/08- Sell 1 x $20 Call @ $2.00

This rolling down strategy generated an additional $180 per contract (200 – 20) into our account.

Analysis:

A consolidating chart pattern deteriorated into a severely declining stock value after November 11th. The total profit generated from the two option sales was $630 (450 + 180). The stock closed @ $19.50, down $7.50 per share or $750 per contract from the original purchase price. Because of the option profits, the net loss was only $120 (750 – 630).

Converting Dead $ To Cash Profits

Situation when converting dead money to cash profits:
We are anywhere in the contract period; market tone is anywhere from positive to negative; and technical analysis of the stock is poor. We simply have had it with the stock as there is no indication of a turnaround.

Example I- AAPL

Charts:

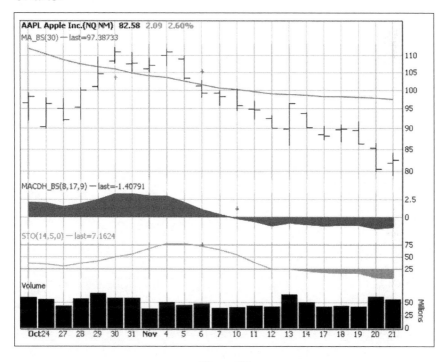

Figure 26

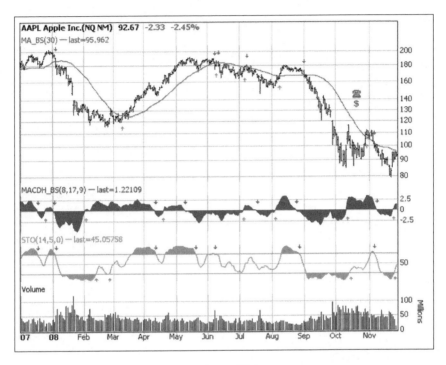

Figure 27

Analysis:

In the above two charts referenced directly above, we see a stock trading under its moving average for 3 months and during the most recent 30 days. Buying back the option during the contract period and then selling the underlying stock allows us to invest in a financial soldier with a healthier technical picture. Many investors tend to hold on to great performers much too long. If you're in the middle of a contract period and find yourself holding onto a stock from the previous cycle performing in a similar fashion as AAPL above, cut your losses…convert dead money to cash profits.

Example 2- BAX

Charts:

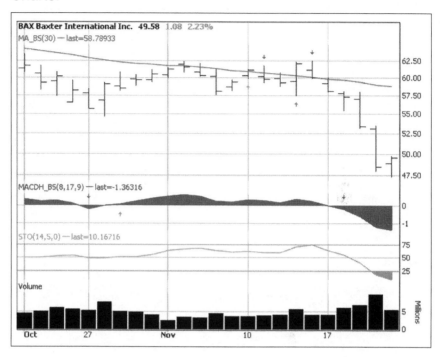

Figure 28

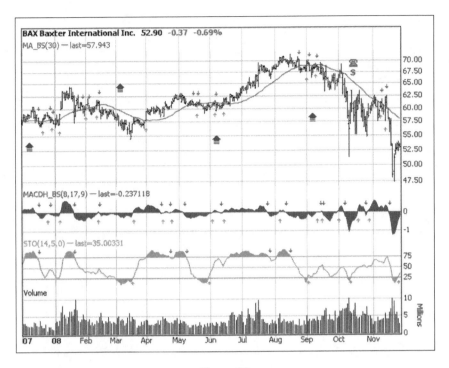

Figure 29

Analysis:

As with the Apple in the preceding example, this was a stock trading under its moving average since September and during the past 30 days. During the final week of the contract period, the equity started dropping precipitously. It was time to buy back the option and convert dead money to cash profits. On the new stock you purchase, it is okay to sell an option for the same month or the following one depending on the calculations. Remember to be aware of earnings reports if you move out to the next month.

Figure 30 on the facing page provides a real life example of how I used this strategy in November of 2006 (the chart is read from the bottom up). I had owned 400 shares of QCOM at an average cost basis of $36.10. I sold two contracts of the $37.50 Calls and two of the

$40 Calls. The share price declined and showed no signs of recovery. The lower two lines on my brokerage statement show that the four contracts were bought back for $46 total (28 +18). Then I proceeded to sell the 400 shares (401 because of dividends) generating a total of $13,923.95. This allowed me to purchase 300 shares of EZPW for $13,617.95, a stock that had a positive technical picture. I then immediately sold the same month option on the replacement equity, gaining $467.93 (3.4%) in profit. Since I bought these shares for $45.37 and sold the $45 call, I lost $111 when these shares were assigned (three contracts @ $37 per contract). Accordingly, my real profit was $356 (467 – 111). This represented a 2.7% 8-day return, cash I never would have earned had I not instituted this exit strategy.

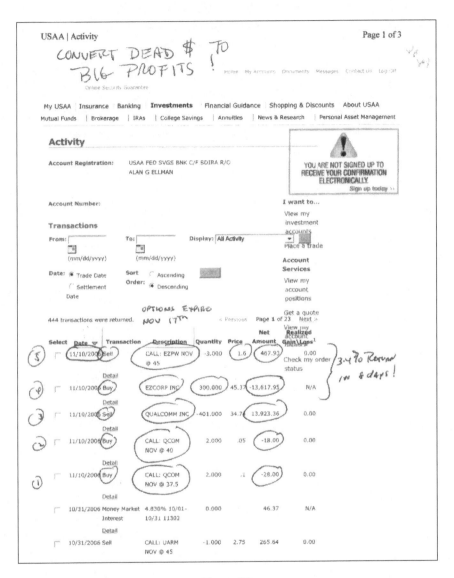

Figure 30

Take No Action

Situation when taking no action:

The stock price has not dropped precipitously so as to meet the 20%/10% threshold rule. Nor are we motivated to sell the stock for fear of a large drop prior to the end of the contract period. The share value holds fairly close to the purchase price but does not surpass the strike price of the sold option. In other words, the best action is no action at all.

Example I- ABT

Charts:

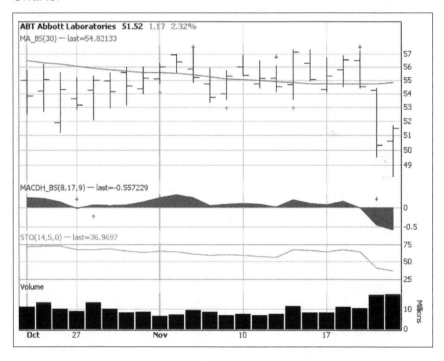

Figure 31

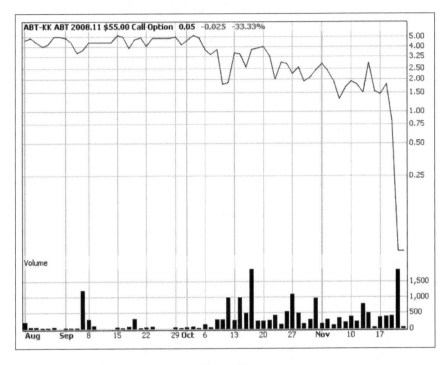

ABT-KK ABT 2008.11 $55.00 Call Option 0.05 -0.025 -33.33%

Figure 32

Calculations:

> 10/20/08- Buy 100 x ABT @ $53.90
> 10/20/08- Sell 1 x $55 Call @ $4.50
> 11/21/08- ABT closes the contract period @ $51.52

Analysis:

There was never a sensible reason to institute an exit strategy during this 5-week contract period as the equity price held fairly steady and closed under the $55 strike price. The stock value declined by $238 ($53.90 - $51.52) for the 100 shares but we earned $450 on the sale of the option. Therefore we profited by $212 (450 – 238) on an investment of $5390 for a 1-month return of 3.9%. After expiration Friday, we determine whether to hold that stock and sell another option the following week, or sell the stock and purchase a different one. This decision will be based on the fundamental and technical analysis of the stock in addition to ensuring that no upcoming earnings report is expected.

Example 2- CHTT

Charts:

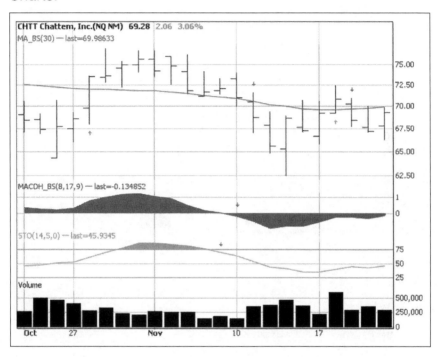

Figure 33

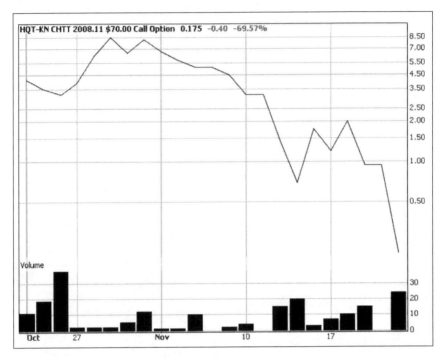

Figure 34

Calculations:

10/20/08- Buy 100 x CHTT @ $68
10/20/08- Sell 1 x 70 Call @ $4
11/21/08- CHTT closes the contract period @ $69.28

Analysis:

This scenario truly is a thing of beauty! The sale of the option generates a 1-month return of 5.9% (400/6800). According to our system criteria for exit strategies pertaining to a 5-week contract period, the option value must drop to .80 (20% of $4) during the first 3 weeks or .40 (10% of $4) during the 4th week. It does not. This example demonstrates the ideal covered call sale scenario as the price of the stock goes up to just below the $70 strike. There is no need for an expiration Friday exit strategy and we are free to sell the next month option if we so choose.

Example 3- GIS

Charts:

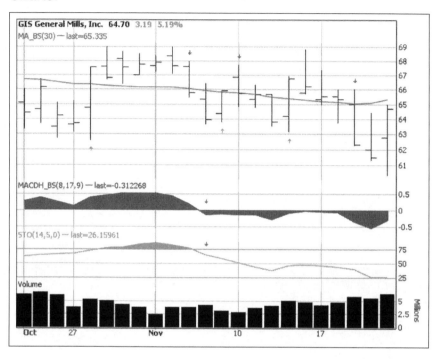

Figure 35

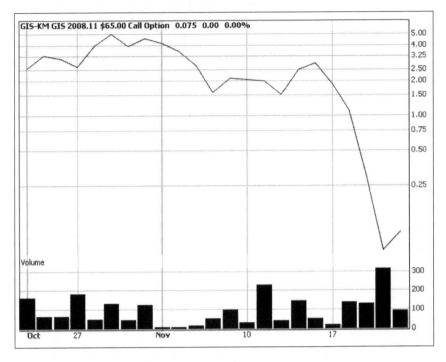

Figure 36

Calculations:

> 10/20/08- Buy 100 x GIS @ $64.40
> 10/20/08- Sell 1 x $65 Call @ $2.50
> 11/21/08- GIS closes the contract period @ $64.70

Analysis:

As with the previous example (CHTT), we have an ideal situation. Our initial option sale generates a 3.9% 1-month return (250/6440). Our option value must drop to .50 (20% of $2.50) during the first 3 weeks or .25 (10% of $2.50) during the 4th week. It does not. The equity value is approximately the same as originally purchased at the beginning of the contract period. We can now determine if the stock meets the system criteria for another option sale in the next period. **Notice on these option charts how premium value *falls off a cliff*** as we approach expiration Friday. This is due to the time decay of the option premium.

Example 4- HCBK

Charts:

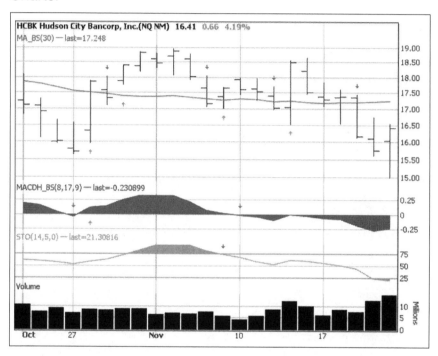

Figure 37

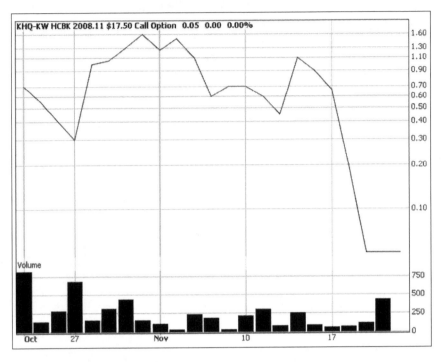

Figure 38

Calculations:

> 10/20/08- Buy 100 x HCBK @ $17.10
> 10/20/08- Sell 1 x $17.50 Call @ .70
> 11/21/08- HCBK closes the contract period @ $16.41

Analysis:

This example demonstrates a situation in which we made no money! We generated $70 per contract on the sale of the option, thereby garnering a 4.1% 1-month profit (70/1710). However, by the end of the contract period the share value had declined by .69 thereby negating our option profit (some investors do not consider the .69 a loss until the shares are sold). HOWEVER, had we not sold the option, we would have incurred a loss rather than break even. **ALL STOCKS WILL NOT GO UP IN VALUE.** By selling covered call options, we are decreasing or negating these losses. As in the previous examples, the option value did not decline to our required 20% or 10% threshold so as to invoke an exit strategy.

Example 5- NVS

Charts:

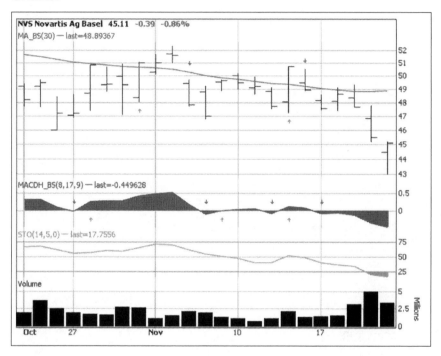

Figure 39

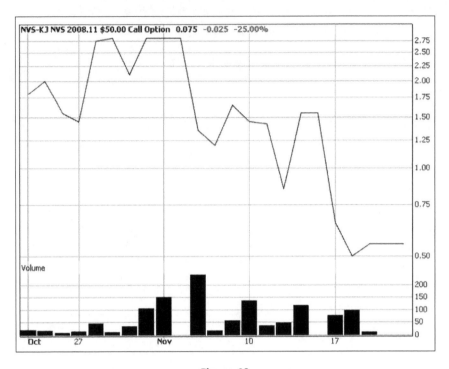

Figure 40

Calculations:

10/20/08- Buy 100 x NVS @ $48.10
10/20/08- Sell 1 x $50 @ $1.80
11/21/08- NVS closes the contract period @ $45.11

Analysis:

As I always say, there IS some risk in selling covered call options. *The risk is in the stock, not in the sale of the option.* In this example, the stock value depreciated $3 per share in one month. At no time in this cycle did the option value fall to the required 20% or 10% level. Now as free-thinking Blue Collar Investors, we could have bought back the option and sold the stock based on the *converting dead money to cash profits* strategy. In this instance, however, I did not, mainly because the bulk of the decline occurred during the last few days. Therefore, the loss was $2.99 per share and the gain for the option sale was $1.80.

This translates to a net loss of $1.19 per share which is a lot more palatable than the loss we would have incurred had we not sold the option.

So there you have it: Three examples which have a happy ending; one demonstrating a neutral outcome; and one resulting in a losing finish. Our objective is to use our system in a manner that yields many more winning scenarios than losing ones, and minimize loss in those situations where a losing scenario is inevitable, through the use of exit strategies.

Hitting a Triple!

Situation when hitting a triple:

We are in the first three to four weeks of the 5-week contract period; market tone is mixed to positive; and technical analysis of the stock is positive. The monthly chart pattern will be volatile as the stock and option values roll up and down.

Rare Example- SLB

Charts:

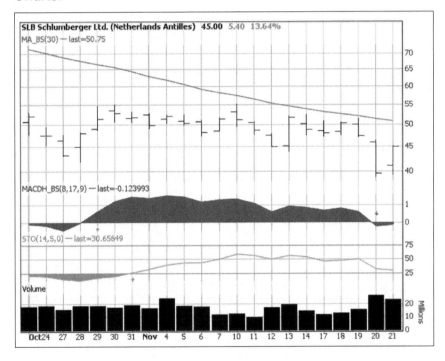

Figure 41

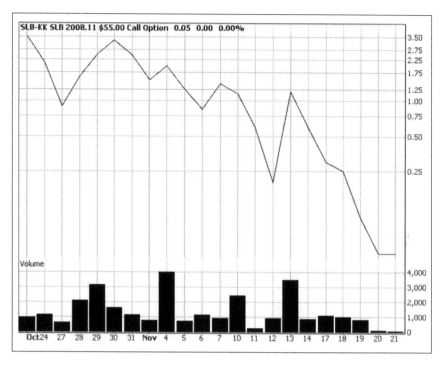

Figure 42

Calculations:

  10/20/08- Buy 100 x SLB @ $52.50
  10/20/08- Sell 1 x $55 Call @ $3.50
  10/27/08- Buy to close the $55 Call @ $.70 (meets our 20% rule)
  10/29/08- Sell 1 $55 Call @ $2.00
  11/12/08- Buy to close the $55 Call @ .20 (meets our 10% rule)
  11/13/08- Sell 1 x $55 Call @ $1.20
  11/21/08- SLB closes the contract period @ $45

Analysis:

On the <u>rare</u> occasions that we *hit a triple*, the chart pattern of the stock looks like a roller-coaster ride. In this case, I bought back the option for the first time by applying the 20% rule @ .70 (20% of $3.50). I sold the same option two days later (lower than the next peak which is hard to predict) for $2.00 giving me an additional profit of $130 per contract

(200 – 70). The option was bought back a second time by applying the 10% rule (now to the $2 premium) for .20 (10% of $2). This time it only took 1 day for the option value to appreciate to $1.20. That third option sale added another $100 per contract (120-20). Our three option premiums collectively came to $670 per contract. We spent $90 per contract to buy back the 2 options (70 + 20). Therefore, our net options profit was $580 per contract. The equity value depreciated by $7.50 per share (52.50 - 45) or $750 per contract so our net loss for the month was $170 per contract (750 - 580). By instituting this exit strategy we turned a potential 14% loss into a much more palatable 3.4% loss. If anyone ever doubts the power of exit strategies, they should be referred to this example. Let me reiterate that triples are extremely rare; doubles are much more commonplace. *If any of you ever hit a triple, let me know and I'll publish it on my website.*

Eleven

Real Life Examples on or near Expiration Friday

Congratulations! When considering expiration Friday exit strategies you are in a great situation. Your stock and option selection has been right on target and now you are deciding whether to keep this equity or allow share assignment. You are very much in the driver's seat!

Take No Action

Situation when taking no action:

In this scenario, the stock price is at or above the strike price and we know that assignment is inevitable if we take no action. Remember, we, as CEOs of our own money, make that determination. Market tone may have turned unfavorable, however it is unlikely that stock technicals are negative since the stock price remained or ascended above the strike price. The two main reasons for taking no action are:

1. An upcoming earnings report (www.earningswhispers.com)

2. Calculations are not favorable and we need to move into a different financial soldier. Using the "*what now*" tab of the ESOC

(Ellman System Options Calculator) will simplify this determination.

In these cases, we simply allow share assignment and use the cash the following week to purchase a different equity to begin cashing in on covered calls.

Example- GHL

Charts:

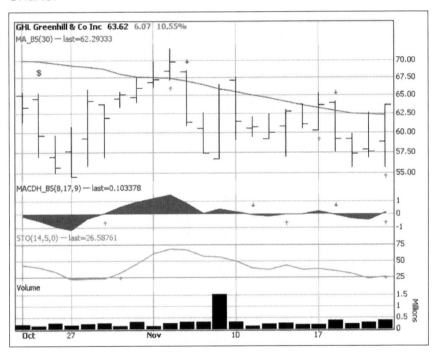

Figure 43

Bk III- GHL Option Chain

Symbol	Last	Intrinsic Value	Bid	Ask	Vol	Open Interest	Strike	Symbol	Last	Intrinsic Value	Bid	Ask	Vol	Open interest
GHL-KK	8.45	8.62	6.90	10.00	30	75	55.00	GHL-WK	0.28	0.00	0.05	0.50	0	60
GHL-KL	3.10	3.62	1.60	4.60	3	64	60.00	GHL-WL	0.47	0.00	0.45	0.50	0	90
GHL-KM	0.05	0.00	0.05	0.05	0	63	65.00	GHL-WM	1.85	1.38	0.60	3.10	0	80
GHL-KN	0.15	0.00	0.05	0.25	0	160	70.00	GHL-WN	6.70	6.38	5.20	8.20	0	40
GHL-KO	0.08	0.00	0.05	0.10	0	106	75.00	GHL-WO	11.70	11.38	10.00	13.40	0	60
GHL-KP	0.23	0.00	0.40	0.05	0	385	80.00	GHL-WP	16.60	16.38	14.80	18.40	0	0
GHL-KQ	0.05	0.00	0.05	0.05	0	41	85.00	GHL-WQ	21.70	21.38	20.00	23.40	0	65

Spreads for Fri Nov 21 21:00:00 PST 2008 Options: Bull Call Spreads | Bull Put Spreads | Bear Call Spreads | Bear Put Spreads

		Calls					Dec 08			Puts				
Symbol	Last	Intrinsic Value	Bid	Ask	Vol	Open Interest	Strike	Symbol	Last	Intrinsic Value	Bid	Ask	Vol	Open interest
GHL-LG	28.40	28.62	26.40	30.40	4	5	35.00	GHL-XG	0.88	0.00	0.10	1.65	0	76
GHL-LH	23.45	23.62	21.40	25.50	0	0	40.00	GHL-XH	1.35	0.00	0.70	2.00	0	88
GHL-LI	18.55	18.62	16.60	20.50	0	0	45.00	GHL-XI	1.50	0.00	0.45	2.55	0	137
GHL-LJ	14.20	13.62	12.20	16.20	3	20	50.00	GHL-XJ	2.77	0.00	0.75	4.80	0	33
GHL-LK	10.15	8.62	8.10	12.20	0	142	55.00	GHL-XK	4.00	0.00	1.80	6.20	0	101
GHL-LL	6.55	3.62	4.70	8.40	0	22	60.00							

Figure 44-GHL Option Chain on Expiration Friday

Calculations:

10/24/08- Stock was purchased for $55.50 (**after the earnings report, noted by the "$" sign**) and the $55 Call option was sold.
11/21/08- GHL closed @ $63.62 at the end of the contract period.

Analysis:

Once the stock was purchased, the share price increased in value and never fell below the initial buy. This eliminated the need for an exit strategy prior to expiration Friday. At this point we assess whether it pays to roll out or roll out and up:

1. *Roll Out-*
   • Buy to close 1 x $55Call @ $10.

- Sell 1 x $55 Call @ $8.10 for a loss of $190 per contract.

2. *Roll out and up-*
    - Buy to close 1 x 55 Call @ $10.
    - Sell 1 $60 Call @ $4.70.
    - This buys up the value of our equity from $55 to $60.00 (your neighbor moving from the kitchen to the dining room).
    - The total value is $9.70 (4.70 + 5 = 9.70).
    - Our loss on this deal is .30 (10 – 9.70).

Both scenarios result in a loss of money. While it is true that both choices offer downside protection, ultimately the name of the game is generating cash into our accounts. Accordingly, in this example we take no action. Our shares are sold automatically over the weekend and the cash is in our account ready to invest into a new warrior to send out into the investment battlefield the following week.

Rolling Out

Situation when rolling out:

The current market value is at or higher than the previously sold strike price, market tone is mixed to positive, stock technicals are mixed to positive, there is no ER coming out in the upcoming contract period, calculations show a good return, and you are uncertain about share appreciation.

Example 1- CHRW

Charts:

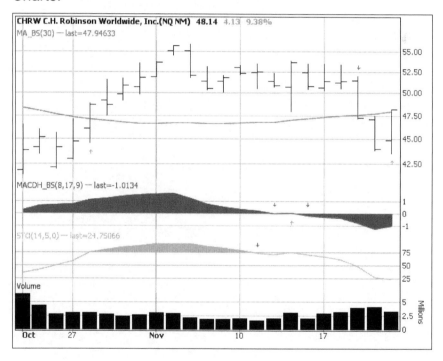

Figure 45

Bk III CHRW Option Chain

Symbol	Last	Intrinsic Value	Bid	Ask	Vol	Open Interest	Strike	Symbol	Last	Intrinsic Value	Bid	Ask	Vol	Open interest
CJQ-KG	13.00	13.14	12.60	13.40	0	64	35.00	CJQ-WG	0.10	0.00	0.05	0.15	0	693
CJQ-KH	8.05	8.14	7.70	8.40	40	503	40.00	CJQ-WH	0.05	0.00	0.05	0.05	0	1,235
CJQ-KI	3.12	3.14	2.85	3.40	848	1,371	45.00	CJQ-WI	0.10	0.00	0.10	0.10	341	1,453
CJQ-KJ	0.10	0.00	0.10	0.10	0	1,605	50.00	CJQ-WJ	1.95	1.86	1.65	2.25	22	4,993
CJQ-KK	0.10	0.00	0.05	0.15	0	1,658	55.00	CJQ-WK	7.05	6.86	6.50	7.60	10	576
CJQ-KL	0.08	0.00	0.05	0.10	0	3,131	60.00	CJQ-WL	12.15	11.86	11.70	12.60	0	786
CJQ-KM	0.08	0.00	0.10	0.05	0	1,530	65.00	CJQ-WM	17.15	16.86	16.70	17.60	0	588
CJQ-KN	0.05	0.00	0.05	0.05	0	560	70.00	CJQ-WN	22.10	21.86	21.60	22.60	0	0
CJQ-KO	0.08	0.00	0.05	0.10	0	300	75.00	CJQ-WO	27.10	26.86	26.60	27.60	0	0
CJQ-KP	0.08	0.00	0.05	0.10	0	438	80.00	CJQ-WP	32.10	31.86	31.60	32.60	0	0
CJQ-KQ	0.08	0.00	0.05	0.10	0	80	85.00	CJQ-WQ	37.05	36.86	36.60	37.50	0	0

Spreads for Fri Nov 21 21:00:00 PST 2008 Options: Bull Call Spreads | Bull Put Spreads | Bear Call Spreads | Bear Put Spreads

	Calls						Dec 08		Puts					
Symbol	Last	Intrinsic Value	Bid	Ask	Vol	Open Interest	Strike	Symbol	Last	Intrinsic Value	Bid	Ask	Vol	Open interest
CJQ-LF	17.35	18.14	16.10	18.60	0	0	30.00	CJQ-XF	0.28	0.00	0.15	0.40	0	51
CJQ-LG	12.80	13.14	11.70	13.90	0	1	35.00	CJQ-XG	0.73	0.00	0.55	0.90	20	21
CJQ-LH	9.20	8.14	8.80	9.60	0	0	40.00	CJQ-XH	1.73	0.00	1.50	1.95	13	111
CJQ-LI	5.55	3.14	5.30	5.80	23	10	45.00	CJQ-XI	3.00	0.00	2.60	3.40	75	64
CJQ-LJ	2.83	0.00	2.55	3.10	325	658	50.00							

Figure 46

Calculations:

10/20/08- Buy 100 x CHRW @ $43 and sell the $45 Call.
11/21/08- CHRW closes the contract period @ $48.14.
11/21/08- Buy to close 1 x $45 Call @ $3.40.
11/21/08- Sell (next month) $45 Call @ $5.30.

Analysis:

As with ALL exit strategies, the initial profit generated from the sale of the option on 10/20/08 has no relevance in the determination of this investment, nor does the original stock purchase price. Since we are required to sell the shares @ $45, our cost basis is $4500 for the

100 shares. Factoring in our initial stock purchase price and option sale profit will only cloud our assessment as to what to do with the $4500 per contract at this point in time. If we buy back the $45 Call for $3.40 and sell the next month $45 Call for $5.30, our net profit is $190 per contract (530 – 340). Since our cost basis is now $4500 (and not what we originally paid for the stock), a 1-month return of 4.2% (190/4500) is generated. This deal also gives us downside protection of $314 (48.14 – 45 per share) or 7% (314/4500). What this means is that we are guaranteed a 1-month profit of 4.2% as long as our share price does not decline by more than 7%. Is that a deal you might be interested in? Me too!

Example 2- DLTR

Charts:

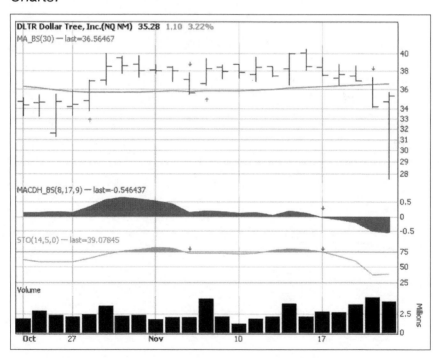

Figure 47

Bk III- DLTR 35 Call

Symbol	Last	Intrinsic Value	Bid	Ask	Vol	Open Interest	Strike	Symbol	Last	Intrinsic Value	Bid	Ask	Vol	Open interest
DQO-KD	15.10	15.28	14.70	15.50	0	18	20.00	DQO-WD	0.08	0.00	0.05	0.10	0	164
DQO-KX	12.70	12.78	12.40	13.00	0	9	22.50	DQO-WX	0.10	0.00	0.05	0.15	0	77
DQO-KE	10.25	10.28	10.00	10.50	5	134	25.00	DQO-WE	0.08	0.00	0.05	0.10	0	654
DQO-KY	7.75	7.78	7.50	8.00	0	107	27.50	DQO-WY	0.08	0.00	0.05	0.10	0	154
DQO-KF	5.25	5.28	5.00	5.50	0	189	30.00	DQO-WF	0.08	0.00	0.05	0.10	0	451
DQO-KZ	2.75	2.78	2.55	2.95	31	473	32.50	DQO-WZ	0.08	0.00	0.05	0.10	24	764
DQO-KG	0.40	0.28	0.20	0.60	155	1,230	35.00	DQO-WG	0.20	0.00	0.15	0.25	115	2,252
DQO-KU	0.05	0.00	0.05	0.05	5	2,775	37.50	DQO-WU	2.25	2.22	2.05	2.45	0	1,208
DQO-KH	0.10	0.00	0.10	0.10	0	2,518	40.00	DQO-WH	4.75	4.72	4.50	5.00	16	1,353
DQO-KV	0.10	0.00	0.05	0.15	0	2,138	42.50	DQO-WV	7.30	7.22	7.00	7.60	0	293
DQO-KI	0.10	0.00	0.05	0.15	0	868	45.00	DQO-WI	9.75	9.72	9.50	10.00	0	36
DQO-KW	0.08	0.00	0.05	0.10	0	265	47.50	DQO-WW	12.30	12.22	12.00	12.60	0	0
DQO-KJ	0.08	0.00	0.05	0.10	0	229	50.00	DQO-WJ	14.80	14.72	14.50	15.10	0	0
DQO-KK	0.08	0.00	0.05	0.10	0	10	55.00	DQO-WK	20.05	19.72	19.50	20.60	0	0

Spreads for Fri Nov 21 21:00:00 PST 2008 Options: Bull Call Spreads | Bull Put Spreads | Bear Call Spreads | Bear Put Spreads

Calls						Dec 08		Puts						
Symbol	Last	Intrinsic Value	Bid	Ask	Vol	Open Interest	Strike	Symbol	Last	Intrinsic Value	Bid	Ask	Vol	Open interest
DQO-LE	10.75	10.28	10.50	11.00	0	0	25.00	DQO-XE	0.50	0.00	0.40	0.60	0	30
DQO-LY	8.55	7.78	8.30	8.80	0	1	27.50	DQO-XY	0.85	0.00	0.80	0.90	2	211
DQO-LF	6.55	5.28	6.30	6.80	0	45	30.00	DQO-XF	1.38	0.00	1.25	1.50	195	231
DQO-LZ	4.75	2.78	4.60	4.90	15	16	32.50	DQO-XZ	2.10	0.00	1.95	2.25	10	174
DQO-LG	3.30	0.28	3.20	3.40	529	1,008	35.00	DQO-XG	3.08	0.00	2.95	3.20	175	928
DQO-LU	2.08	0.00	1.95	2.20	116	392	37.50	DQO						

Figure 48

Calculations:

10/20/08- Buy 100 x DLTR @ $34.25 and sell $35 Call option.
11/21/08- DLTR closes the contract period @ $35.28.
11/21/08- Buy to close $35 call @ .60.
11/21/08- Sell (next month) $35 call @ $3.20.

Analysis:

When a stock is purchased just below a strike price and ends the contract period slightly above that strike, most of the time you will institute a rolling out exit strategy (if all system criteria are met). Rolling out and up will occur more frequently when the share price is significantly higher than the original strike. That's not the case here. Our cost basis is $3500 since that is what we would get if we *allow* assignment. Our package of a .60 buy to close and a $3.20 option sale leaves us with a net profit of $260 per contract. This results in a 7.4% 1-month return (260/3500). We do have small downside protection of $28 per contract but this amount is negligible I would not factor it into my investment decision.

Example 3- DV

Charts:

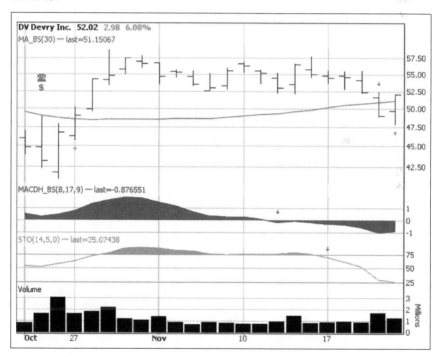

Figure 49

Bk III- DV Option Chain   NOV. 108

Symbol	Last	Intrinsic Value	Bid	Ask	Vol	Open Interest	Strike	Symbol	Last	Intrinsic Value	Bid	Ask	Vol	Open interest
DV-KE	26.15	27.02	25.10	27.20	0	1	25.00	DV-WE	0.10	0.00	0.10	0.10	0	72
DV-KF	21.20	22.02	20.10	22.30	0	0	30.00	DV-WF	0.08	0.00	0.05	0.10	0	76
DV-KG	16.20	17.02	15.10	17.30	1	12	35.00	DV-WG	0.05	0.00	0.05	0.05	0	570
DV-KH	11.20	12.02	10.20	12.20	2	84	40.00	DV-WH	0.08	0.00	0.05	0.10	0	2,193
DV-KI	6.45	7.02	5.60	7.30	1	484	45.00	DV-WI	0.20	0.00	0.25	0.15	2	499
DV-KJ	1.77	2.02	1.30	2.25	108	645	50.00	DV-WJ	0.15	0.00	0.15	0.15	183	647
DV-KK	0.20	0.00	0.30	0.10	0	1,482	55.00	DV-WK	3.62	2.98	2.85	4.40	2	166
DV-KL	0.05	0.00	0.05	0.05	2	644	60.00	DV-WL	8.60	7.98	7.80	9.40	0	124
DV-KM	0.08	0.00	0.05	0.10	2	545	65.00	DV-WM	13.85	12.98	12.80	14.90	0	50
DV-KN	0.10	0.00	0.10	0.10	0	98	70.00	DV-WN	18.85	17.98	17.80	19.90	0	0
DV-KO	0.08	0.00	0.05	0.10	0	74	75.00	DV-WO	23.85	22.98	22.80	24.90	0	0
DV-KP	0.08	0.00	0.05	0.10	0	153	80.00	DV-WP	28.85	27.98	27.70	30.00	0	0
DV-KQ	0.08	0.00	0.05	0.10	0	69	85.00	DV-WQ	33.85	32.98	32.80	34.90	0	0
DV-KR	0.08	0.00	0.05	0.10	0	0	90.00	DV-WR	38.80	37.98	37.70	39.90	0	0
DV-KS	0.08	0.00	0.05	0.10	0	10	95.00	DV-WS	43.85	42.98	42.70	45.00	0	0

Spreads for Fri Nov 21 21:00:00 PST 2008 Options: Bull Call Spreads | Bull Put Spreads | Bear Call Spreads | Bear Put Spreads

	Calls						Dec 08		Puts					
Symbol	Last	Intrinsic Value	Bid	Ask	Vol	Open Interest	Strike	Symbol	Last	Intrinsic Value	Bid	Ask	Vol	Open interest
DV-LG	16.75	17.02	15.70	17.80	0	10	35.00	DV-XG	0.55	0.00	0.40	0.70	2	37
DV-LH	12.40	12.02	11.60	13.20	0	5	40.00	DV-XH	1.02	0.00	0.85	1.20	2	27
DV-LI	8.25	7.02	7.60	8.90	0	0	45.00	DV-XI	1.88	0.00	1.60	2.15	20	67
DV-LJ	4.70	2.02	4.20	5.20	13	144	50.00	DV-XJ	3.45	0.00	3.00	3.90	25	43
DV-LK	2.17	0.00	1.80	2.55	140	332	55.00	DV-XK	5.80	2.98	5.30	6.30	0	169

Figure 50

Calculations:

10/23/08- Buy 100 x DV @ $47.40 (**after the earnings report**) and sell the $50 Call.

11/21/08- DV closes the contract period @ $52.02.

11/21/08- Buy to close the $50 Call @ $2.25 (buy at the *ask;* the higher figure).

11/21/08- Sell the next month $50 Call @ $4.20 (sell at the bid; the lower figure).

Analysis:

After determining that this equity is eligible for an expiration Friday exit strategy, we look at the numbers to determine the quality of financial soldier DV will be in the upcoming contract period. Our only loyalty is to the cash generated into our account, not to the vehicle carrying those funds. Buying back the $50 Call will cost us $2.25. This makes sense since we have $2.02 in intrinsic value (52.02 – 50) and a little bit of time value (in this case .23 which includes money for the market makers). To roll out to the next month's same strike, we generate $4.20 per share or $420 per contract. Our net profit is $195 (420 – 225). Our cost basis is $5000 because if we allow assignment that is the amount of cash it will generate into our account, not $5202. Therefore, our 1-month return is 3.9% (195/5000) with a downside protection of 4% (202/5000). This means that we are guaranteed a 1-month return of 3.9% as long as our shares do not decline by more than 4%. Are you in or out?

Rolling Out and Up

Situation when rolling out and up:

We use the rolling out and up strategy when the current market value is at or more than the previously sold strike price, market tone is mixed to positive, stock technicals are positive, there is no ER coming out in the upcoming contract period, calculations show a good return, and you are relatively confident about share appreciation. This is a more bullish maneuver than simply rolling out.

Example 1- APOL: Rolling Out and Up/At-the-Money

Charts:

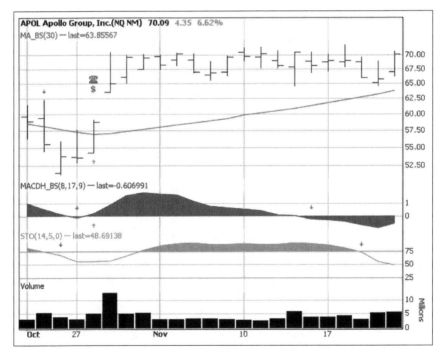

Figure 51

APOL Option Chain   NOV 08

Symbol	Last	Intrinsic Value	Bid	Ask	Vol	Open Interest	Strike	Symbol	Last	Intrinsic Value	Bid	Ask	Vol	Open interest
OAQ-KD	50.05	50.09	49.80	50.30	0	21	20.00	OAQ-WD	0.08	0.00	0.05	0.10	0	140
OAQ-KX	47.60	47.59	47.40	47.80	0	32	22.50	OAQ-WX	0.08	0.00	0.05	0.10	0	46
OAQ-KE	45.05	45.09	44.80	45.30	0	45	25.00	OAQ-WE	0.08	0.00	0.05	0.10	0	371
OAQ-KF	40.05	40.09	39.80	40.30	0	18	30.00	OAQ-WF	0.08	0.00	0.05	0.10	1	437
OAQ-KG	35.05	35.09	34.80	35.30	2	59	35.00	OAQ-WG	0.05	0.00	0.05	0.05	0	839
OAQ-KH	30.05	30.09	29.80	30.30	0	141	40.00	OAQ-WH	0.08	0.00	0.05	0.10	0	1,941
OAQ-KI	25.05	25.09	24.80	25.30	65	391	45.00	OAQ-WI	0.05	0.00	0.05	0.05	0	2,958
OAQ-KJ	20.05	20.09	19.80	20.30	129	1,676	50.00	OAQ-WJ	0.05	0.00	0.05	0.05	11	5,555
OAQ-KK	15.05	15.09	14.80	15.30	94	3,095	55.00	OAQ-WK	0.05	0.00	0.05	0.05	0	5,900
OAQ-KL	10.10	10.09	9.90	10.30	449	5,097	60.00	OAQ-WL	0.05	0.00	0.05	0.05	70	6,518
OAQ-KM	5.10	5.09	4.90	(5.30)	58	5,536	65.00	OAQ-WM	0.05	0.00	0.05	0.05	1,247	4,714
OAQ-KN	0.30	0.09	0.15	0.45	1,726	5,548	70.00	OAQ-WN	0.20	0.00	0.30	0.10	79	2,048
OAQ-KO	0.08	0.00	0.05	0.10	10	4,103	75.00	OAQ-WO	4.95	4.91	4.70	5.20	0	396
OAQ-KP	0.08	0.00	0.05	0.10	0	973	80.00	OAQ-WP	9.95	9.91	9.70	10.20	10	133
OAQ-KQ	0.08	0.00	0.05	0.10	0	856	85.00	OAQ-WQ	14.95	14.91	14.70	15.20	0	10
OAQ-KR	0.08	0.00	0.05	0.10	0	137	90.00	OAQ-WR	19.95	19.91	19.70	20.20	0	24
OAQ-KS	0.08	0.00	0.05	0.10	0	61	95.00	OAQ-WS	24.95	24.91	24.70	25.20	0	0
OAQ-KT	0.08	0.00	0.05	0.10	0	30	100.00	OAQ-WT	29.95	29.91	29.70	30.20	0	0
OAQ-KA	0.08	0.00	0.05	0.10	0	25	105.00	OAQ-WA	34.90	34.91	34.70	35.10	0	0
OAQ-KB	0.10	0.00	N/A	0.10	0	0	110.00	OAQ-WB	39.95	39.91	39.70	40.20	0	0

Spreads for Fri Nov 21 21:00:00 PST 2008 Options: Bull Call Spreads | Bull Put Spreads | Bear Call Spreads | Bear Put Spreads

	Calls						Dec 08		Puts					
Symbol	Last	Intrinsic Value	Bid	Ask	Vol	Open Interest	Strike	Symbol	Last	Intrinsic Value	Bid	Ask	Vol	Open interest
OAQ-LG	34.75	35.09	34.10	35.40	0	10	35.00	OAQ-XG	0.10	0.00	0.05	0.15	3	194
OAQ-LH	30.25	30.09	30.00	30.50	0	14	40.00	OAQ-XH	0.15	0.00	0.10	0.20	1	278
OAQ-LI	25.40	25.09	25.20	25.60	11	2	45.00	OAQ-XI	0.33	0.00	0.25	0.40	6	599
OAQ-LJ	20.70	20.09	20.50	20.90	203	423	50.00	OAQ-XJ	0.68	0.00	0.60	0.75	549	582
OAQ-LK	16.30	15.09	16.10	16.50	0	629	55.00	OAQ-XK	1.23	0.00	1.15	1.30	45	790
OAQ-LL	12.20	10.09	12.00	12.40	15	1,289	60.00	OAQ-XL	2.12	0.00	2.00	2.25	1,553	4,924
OAQ-LM	8.55	5.09	8.40	8.70	120	1,235	65.00	OAQ-XM	3.45	0.00	3.30	3.60	598	2,603
OAQ-LN	5.50	0.09	(5.30)	5.70	685	3,560	70.00	OAQ-XN	5.50	0.00	5.40	5.60	325	2,627

figure 52

Calculations:

> 10/29/08- Buy 100 x APOL @ $65 (**after the earnings report**) and sell
> the $65 Call.
> 11/21/08- APOL closes the contract period @ $70.09.
> 11/21/08- Buy to close the $65 Call @ $5.30.
> 11/21/08- Sell the next month $70 Call @ $5.30.

Analysis:

In this instance, we are rolling out and up to an at-the-money strike since the .09 difference is negligible in our calculations. The option buy-back and subsequent sale is a wash, so no profit is generated from the options aspect of this transaction. However, our stock value is bought-up from $65 to $70 per share. If we do not institute an expiration Friday exit strategy, our shares will be sold for the agreed upon price of $65. This is the obligation we undertook when we sold the original option. Therefore, $6500 is our cost basis when comparing this choice to others (using the $6500 to buy another stock and sell the option on the new one). By rolling out and up to the $70 Call, our shares are now worth $5 per share more or $500 per contract. Using our previous analogy, we are walking our neighbor from our kitchen with a 65 inch high ceiling into our dining room which has a 70 inch ceiling. Now our neighbor, who is 70.09 inches tall measures 70 inches from head to toe instead of the 65 inches he measured in our kitchen. $500 is $500 no matter where it comes from so we need to compute that into our investment decisions. Our 1-month return is 7.7% (500/6500) with no downside protection or upside potential. Remember rolling out and up is an extremely bullish strategy and that is precisely the reason we insist that technicals are positive before employing this choice. Although I say that there is no downside protection, there is another way to look at this example. What if your equity does drop in value by 4% in this 1-month contract period? Now your profit drops to 3.7% (7.7 – 4) for the 30-days. Folks, that annualizes out to 44%! No Kleenex needed!

Example 2- CPO: Rolling Out and Up/Out-of-the-Money

Charts:

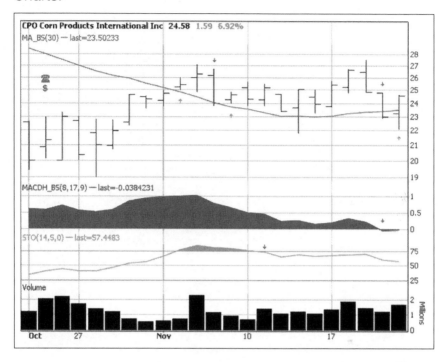

Figure 53

Bk III CPO Option Chain

Nov 08

Symbol	Last	Intrinsic Value	Bid	Ask	Vol	Open Interest	Strike	Symbol	Last	Intrinsic Value	Bid	Ask	Vol	Open interest
CPO-KW	7.00	7.08	6.40	7.60	0	39	17.50	CPO-WW	0.20	0.00	0.05	0.35	0	235
CPO-KD	4.55	4.58	4.10	5.00	1	803	20.00	CPO-WD	0.25	0.00	0.15	0.35	0	314
CPO-KX	2.25	2.08	2.05	2.45	6	265	22.50	CPO-WX	0.22	0.00	0.10	0.35	0	76
CPO-KE	0.10	0.00	0.15	0.05	0	764	25.00	CPO-WE	0.65	0.42	0.30	1.00	5	318
CPO-KF	0.22	0.00	0.10	0.35	0	326	30.00	CPO-WF	5.60	5.42	5.10	6.10	0	3
CPO-KG	0.05	0.00	0.05	0.05	0	34	35.00	CPO-WG	10.70	10.42	10.10	11.30	0	0
CPO-KH	0.05	0.00	0.05	0.05	0	34	40.00	CPO-WH	15.80	15.42	15.00	16.60	0	0
CPO-KI	0.25	0.00	0.15	0.35	0	0	45.00	CPO-WI	20.75	20.42	19.90	21.60	0	0

Spreads for Fri Nov 21 21:00:00 PST 2008 Options: Bull Call Spreads | Bull Put Spreads | Bear Call Spreads | Bear Put Spreads

		Calls					Dec 08	Puts						
Symbol	Last	Intrinsic Value	Bid	Ask	Vol	Open Interest	Strike	Symbol	Last	Intrinsic Value	Bid	Ask	Vol	Open interest
CPO-LC	9.70	9.58	9.20	10.20	0	0	15.00	CPO-XC	0.35	0.00	0.15	0.55	2	21
CPO-LW	7.40	7.08	6.80	8.00	0	3	17.50	CPO-XW	0.62	0.00	0.40	0.85	5	47
CPO-LD	5.60	4.58	5.20	6.00	5	64	20.00	CPO-XD	1.10	0.00	0.90	1.30	8	49
CPO-LX	3.80	2.08	3.40	4.20	0	54	22.50	CPO-XX	1.90	0.00	1.65	2.15	603	74
CPO-LE	2.45	0.00	2.10	2.80	20	22	25.00							

Figure 54

Calculations:

10/24/08: Buy 100 x CPO @ $23 (**after the earnings report**) and sell
the $22.50 Call option
11/21/08- CPO closes the contract period @ $24.58
11/21/08- Buy to close 1 x $22.50 Call @ $2.45
11/21/08- Sell 1 x $25 call @ $2.10

Analysis:

The closing of the current option position with the subsequent sale of
the next month's higher strike, results in a loss of .35 (2.45 – 2.10). The
elevation of the strike price from $22.50 to $25 buys up the share value
from $22.50 to $24.58 or by $2.08. Therefore, our net profit from this
transaction is $1.73 per share (2.08 - .35) or $173 per contract. This
calculates to a 1-month return of 7.7% (173/2250) with an upside po-

tential of 1.9% (42/2250). When you sell an out-of-the-money strike, the upside potential is the difference between the strike (25) and the current market value of the equity (24.58).

Example 3- DV: Rolling Out and Up/ In-the-Money

Charts:

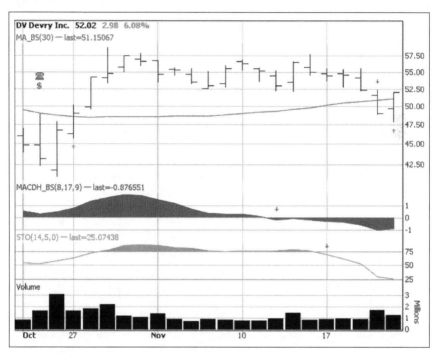

Figure 55

Bk III- DV Option Chain — NOV. 108

Symbol	Last	Intrinsic Value	Bid	Ask	Vol	Open Interest	Strike	Symbol	Last	Intrinsic Value	Bid	Ask	Vol	Open interest
DV-KE	26.15	27.02	25.10	27.20	0	1	25.00	DV-WE	0.10	0.00	0.10	0.10	0	72
DV-KF	21.20	22.02	20.10	22.30	0	0	30.00	DV-WF	0.08	0.00	0.05	0.10	0	76
DV-KG	16.20	17.02	15.10	17.30	1	12	35.00	DV-WG	0.05	0.00	0.05	0.05	0	570
DV-KH	11.20	12.02	10.20	12.20	2	84	40.00	DV-WH	0.08	0.00	0.05	0.10	0	2,193
DV-KI	6.45	7.02	5.60	7.30	1	48	45.00	DV-WI	0.20	0.00	0.25	0.15	2	499
DV-KJ	1.77	2.02	1.30	2.25	108	645	50.00	DV-WJ	0.15	0.00	0.15	0.15	183	647
DV-KK	0.20	0.00	0.30	0.10	0	1,482	55.00	DV-WK	3.62	2.98	2.85	4.40	2	166
DV-KL	0.05	0.00	0.05	0.05	2	644	60.00	DV-WL	8.60	7.98	7.80	9.40	0	124
DV-KM	0.08	0.00	0.05	0.10	2	545	65.00	DV-WM	13.85	12.98	12.80	14.90	0	50
DV-KN	0.10	0.00	0.10	0.10	0	98	70.00	DV-WN	18.85	17.98	17.80	19.90	0	0
DV-KO	0.08	0.00	0.05	0.10	0	74	75.00	DV-WO	23.85	22.98	22.80	24.90	0	0
DV-KP	0.08	0.00	0.05	0.10	0	153	80.00	DV-WP	28.85	27.98	27.70	30.00	0	0
DV-KQ	0.08	0.00	0.05	0.10	0	69	85.00	DV-WQ	33.85	32.98	32.80	34.90	0	0
DV-KR	0.08	0.00	0.05	0.10	0	0	90.00	DV-WR	38.80	37.98	37.70	39.90	0	0
DV-KS	0.08	0.00	0.05	0.10	0	10	95.00	DV-WS	43.85	42.98	42.70	45.00	0	0

Spreads for Fri Nov 21 21:00:00 PST 2008 Options: Bull Call Spreads | Bull Put Spreads | Bear Call Spreads | Bear Put Spreads

		Calls				Dec 08				Puts				
Symbol	Last	Intrinsic Value	Bid	Ask	Vol	Open Interest	Strike	Symbol	Last	Intrinsic Value	Bid	Ask	Vol	Open interest
DV-LG	16.75	17.02	15.70	17.80	0	10	35.00	DV-XG	0.55	0.00	0.40	0.70	2	37
DV-LH	12.40	12.02	11.60	13.20	0	5	40.00	DV-XH	1.02	0.00	0.85	1.20	2	27
DV-LI	8.25	7.02	7.60	8.90	0	0	45.00	DV-XI	1.88	0.00	1.60	2.15	20	67
DV-LJ	4.70	2.02	4.20	5.20	13	144	50.00	DV-XJ	3.45	0.00	3.00	3.90	25	43
DV-LK	2.17	0.00	1.80	2.55	140	332	55.00	DV-XK	5.80	2.98	5.30	6.30	0	169
D														

Figure 56

Calculations:

10/23/08- Buy 100 x DV @ $47.40 (**after the earnings report**) and
   sell the $45 Call

11/21/08- DV closes the contract period @ $52.02

11/21/08- Buy to close 1 x $45 Call @ $7.30

11/21/08- Sell next month's $50 Call for $4.20

Analysis:

The original $45 call was sold to garner downside protection. It turns out that we didn't need this downside protection as the stock increased in value. Understand that we still made a GREAT 1-month return even on this in-the-money strike. Now we are faced with the decision as to whether to execute an expiration Friday exit strategy. With all the technicals confirming positive (a situation we are assuming), we consider rolling out and up. In this instance, we lose $3.10 per share on the options aspect of the transaction (7.30 – 4.20). However, we gain $5.00 per share by buying up the share value from the $45 agreed upon sales price to the new strike of $50. The net on this transaction computes to + $1.90 per share or + $190 per contract. Since our cost basis is $4500, the 1-month return is 4.2% (190/4500) with a downside protection of 3.9% (202/5202). Therefore, for this deal, we are guaranteed a 1-month return of 4.2% as long as the equity value does not diminish by more than 4.5%. This, along with many of the other examples, highlights the importance of factoring in stock appreciation, upside potential and downside protection in our investment decisions. Had we only looked at the options aspect of this deal, we would have run for the hills after we calculated a loss of $310 per contract. However, as educated Blue Collar Investors, we know better!

Thus far, we have evaluated the different exit strategies available to us under various particular sets of circumstances. We then either decide to take no action or select the best exit strategy available. In addition to these situations, there are occasions when we can utilize multiple exit strategies for the same stock in the same contract period. Chapter 12 will explore some of these opportunities.

Twelve

Using Multiple Exit Strategies in the Same Contract Period

Selling a covered call stock option does NOT create an opportunity to fall asleep until the end of the contract period. This notion is implicit in utilizing exit strategies; when we execute an exit strategy, we still must remain alert, as we may benefit from a second or third exit strategy on that same stock in the same month. To some extent, we have already seen this when we hit a triple or rolled down two times. In those instances, we used multiple exit strategies of the same kind. In this chapter, we will review examples of using different types of exit strategies for the same stocks in the same month. This really isn't that complicated. All it means is that once you've executed an exit strategy, treat it as if you are starting all over with this new investment situation, and stay on the alert for another possible exit strategy. Some of these situations will enhance our profits, while others will diminish losses; either way, tremendous rewards will result, particularly considering the amount of time spent making these decisions. Remember, what may seem complicated initially, will become second nature to you once mastered. In this chapter I will highlight two situations wherein we execute multiple exit strategies for the same stock in the same contract period.

Example 1- NAV: Hitting a Double and Rolling Down

Charts:

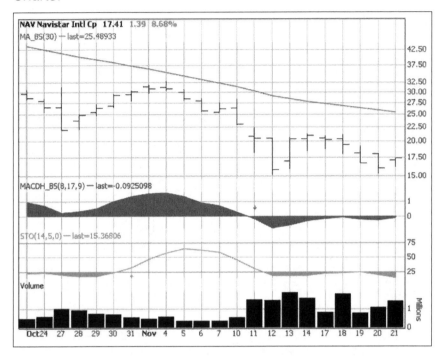

Figure 57

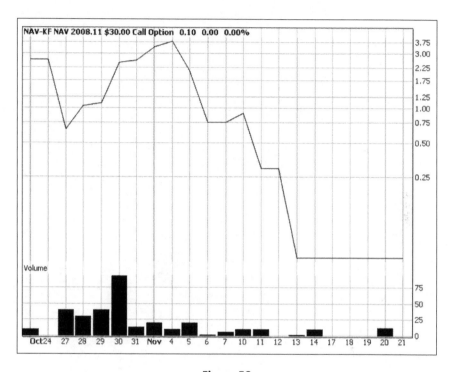

Figure 58

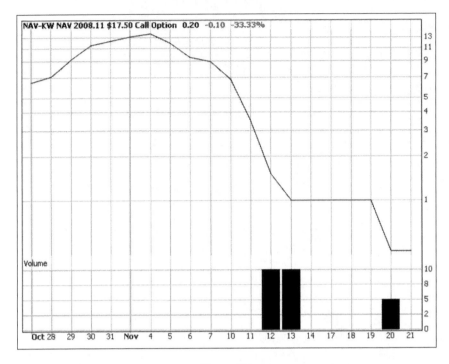

Figure 59

Calculations:

> 10/20/08- Buy 100 x NAV @ $29
> 10/20/08- Sell 1 x $30 call @ $2.75
> 10/27/08- Buy to close 1 x $30 Call @ .55 (meets our 20% rule)
> 10/31/08- Sell 1 x $30 Call @ $2.75
> 11/12/08- Buy to close 1 x $30 call @ .30 (approximates our 10% rule)
> 11/12/08- Roll down and sell 1 $17.50 call @ $1.00
> 11/21/08- NAV closes the contract period @ $17.41

Analysis:

It's only fair that I show you a stock suffering from cardiac arrest in major need of CPR! This financial soldier fooled me, as it had great fundamentals and technicals, yet, still fell off a cliff after November 4th. In the earlier part of the contract period, the stock went down and then up in value. That allowed me to hit a double by buying-to-close my option position on October 27th and reselling the same option on October 31st. After that, all %$*&% broke loose! On November 12th, I bought back the option at .30 (close to the required 10% of the $2.75 sale). This financial warrior, now on life-support, closed that day at $16 per share. I rolled down to the $17.50 strike to generate an additional $100 per contract and salvage what I could. The stock value declined from $29 to $17.41 in one month, a loss of $1159 per contract. Let's see how the option exit strategies took some of the bite out of this one:

Profits: The three option sales totaled $650 (275 + 275 + 100).
Losses: Option buy-to-close costs totaled .85 (.55 + .30) or $85 per contract.

- Share loss for 100 units was $1159 (29 – 17.41 per share).
- Total losses were $1244 (1159 + 85).

When factoring in the profits generated from the multiple exit strategies, my losses decreased to $594 (1244 – 650), thereby cutting losses by more than half. Although losing almost $600 is no reason to celebrate, I'm sure you'll all agree that it's much better than a loss of nearly $1200. Some of our equities will go down in value, and even may fall off a cliff as NAV did in this case. We must be prepared to execute an exit strategy, potentially even multiple exit strategies, in the same contract period, to minimize our losses.

Example 2- MVL: Rolling Down and Rolling Out

Charts:

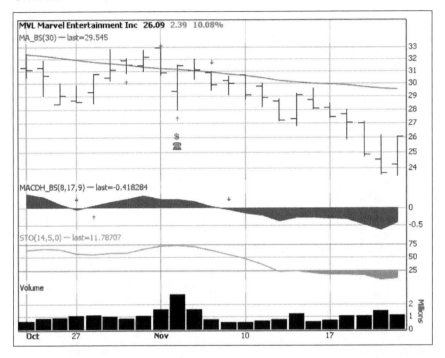

Figure 60

Figure 61

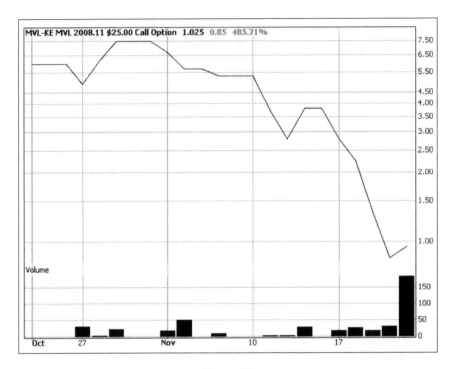

Figure 62

Bk III- MVL Option Chain   Nov 08

Symbol	Last	Intrinsic Value	Bid	Ask	Vol	Open Interest	Strike	Symbol	Last	Intrinsic Value	Bid	Ask	Vol	Open interest
MVL-KD	6.05	6.09	5.90	6.20	0	0	20.00	MVL-WD	0.05	0.00	N/A	0.05	0	0
MVL-KX	3.50	3.59	3.30	3.70	0	200	22.50	MVL-WX	0.10	0.00	0.15	0.05	0	0
MVL-KE	1.02	1.09	0.85	1.20	184	93	25.00	MVL-WE	0.05	0.00	0.05	0.05	31	639
MVL-KF	0.05	0.00	0.05	0.05	3	440	30.00	MVL-WF	4.00	3.91	3.80	4.20	2	362
MVL-KG	0.05	0.00	0.05	0.05	4	1,012	35.00	MVL-WG	9.00	8.91	8.80	9.20	0	48
MVL-KH	0.05	0.00	0.05	0.05	0	332	40.00	MVL-WH	13.95	13.91	13.80	14.10	0	4
MVL-KI	0.05	0.00	0.05	0.05	0	3	45.00	MVL-WI	18.95	18.91	18.80	19.10	0	0

Spreads for Fri Nov 21 21:00:00 PST 2008 Options: Bull Call Spreads | Bull Put Spreads | Bear Call Spreads | Bear Put Spreads

	Calls						Dec 08		Puts					
Symbol	Last	Intrinsic Value	Bid	Ask	Vol	Open Interest	Strike	Symbol	Last	Intrinsic Value	Bid	Ask	Vol	Open interest
MVL-LW	8.75	8.59	8.50	9.00	0	0	17.50	MVL-XW	0.28	0.00	0.20	0.35	0	10
MVL-LD	6.45	6.09	6.20	6.70	0	0	20.00	MVL-XD	0.50	0.00	0.45	0.55	0	11
MVL-LX	4.45	3.59	4.30	4.60	0	61	22.50	MVL-XX	0.90	0.00	0.85	0.95	152	592
MVL-LE	2.67	1.09	2.60	2.75	412	480	25.00	MVL-XE	1.75	0.00	1.65	1.85	45	10,321
MVL-LF	0.75	0.00	0.65	0.85	330	1,456	30.00							

Figure 63

Calculations:

11/7/08- Buy 100 x MVL @ $31.10 (**after the earnings report**)
11/7/08- Sell 1 x $30 Call @ $2.50
11/11/08- Buy to close 1 x $30 Call @ .25 (meets our 10% rule)
11/11/08- Sell 1 x $25 Call @ $2.90
11/21/08- MVL closes the contract period @ $26.09
11/21/08- Buy to close 1 x $25 Call @ $1.20
11/21/08- Sell 1 x (next month) $25 Call @ $2.60

Analysis:

This is an interesting example in that the earnings report came out midway through the contract period (see the $ sign on the stock chart). Our system criteria prohibit us from selling options prior to this report so we must wait until after the announcement to jump in. With only two weeks remaining in the contract period the stock was purchased and an option sold. Shortly thereafter, the equity started declining in value, and on November 11[th,] the option value declined to 10% of the original option sale (.25), enabling us to roll down to the next lower strike, $25. On expiration Friday, MVL closes above that second strike price so we instituted an expiration Friday exit strategy to roll out. Since the initial option sale ($30 strike) was in-the-money, the stock purchase was *bought down* to the $30 strike figure (see Chapter 9 of my book, *Cashing in on Covered Calls*). This transaction resulted in an option profit of $140 per contract (250 − 110) on this first sale. The roll down exit strategy resulted in a net profit of $265 per contract (290 - 25). Therefore, for the current contract period, the option profit was $405 (140 + 265). Our obligation to sell @ $25 means we lost $5 per share in stock value (30 − 25) or $500 per contract. The net loss for the month was $95 (500 − 405); much more palatable than the $391 ($30 - $26.09) loss we would have incurred had we not sold options and utilized exit strategies. Now, computing the profit for the next contract cycle, we buy back the $25 Call ($120 per contract) and sell the next month's $25 call ($260 per contract). This results in a net profit of $140 and a 5.6% 1-month return (140/2500). We also capture a downside protection of 4.4% (109/2500). In other words, we are guaranteed a 5.6% 1-month return as long as our shares do not depreciate in value by more than 4.4% in that contract period. This example clearly demonstrates how exit strategy utilization can significantly decrease losses and generate tremendous monthly profits.

Now that we have analyzed examples of all the different types of exit strategies, the next chapter will discuss how the ESOC (Ellman System Options Calculator) will make the mathematics aspect a non-issue even for the mathematically-challenged!

Thirteen

The Ellman System Options Calculator

Over the past few years, when giving my seminars, computing option returns has been *the* major headache for Blue Collar Investors. Fortunately, that problem is no longer an issue as we have the Ellman System Options Calculator (ESOC). I developed this instrument along with Owen Sargent, an outstanding accountant and seasoned stock market investor.

The calculator is set up with four tabs on the lower left portion of the page:

1. **Intro**- Highlights general information about the calculation process.

2. **Single**- Allows you to evaluate returns from different strikes for the same stock.

3. **Multiple**- Compare returns, upside potential, and downside protection for many stocks, all on the same page.

4. **WHAT NOW**- Calculates the returns for a package transaction where an option is bought back and another is sold.

Single Tab

RETURN ON OPTION (ROO) CALCULATOR - SINGLE STOCK

Stock name >>	APPLE COMPUTER			
Stock symbol >>	AAPL		Stock share price >>	$ 94.00

	Symbol	Strike Price	Exp Date	Price / share
Option choice #1 >>	QAA AR	90.00	01/16/09	11.25
Option choice #2 >>	QAA AS	95.00	01/16/09	8.55
Option choice #3 >>	QAA AT	100.00	01/16/09	6.30
Option choice #4 >>	QAA AA	105.00	01/16/09	4.50

Option selected	AAPL JAN 90.00	AAPL JAN 95.00	AAPL JAN 100.00	AAPL JAN 105.00
Today's date	12/08/08	12/08/08	12/08/08	12/08/08
Days to expiration	39	39	39	39
Cost for 100 shares of stock	$ 9,400.00	$ 9,400.00	$ 9,400.00	$ 9,400.00
Proceeds from one contract	$ 1,125.00	$ 855.00	$ 630.00	$ 450.00

IN / OUT OF THE MONEY	IN	OUT	OUT	OUT
INTRINSIC VALUE	$ 4.00	$ -	$ -	$ -
UPSIDE AMOUNT	$ -	$ 100.00	$ 600.00	$ 1,100.00
UPSIDE POTENTIAL	0.0%	1.1%	6.4%	11.7%
DOWNSIDE AMOUNT	$ 400.00	$ -	$ -	$ -
DOWNSIDE PROTECTION	4.3%	0.0%	0.0%	0.0%

RETURN ON VARIOUS OUTCOMES				
Proceeds from option sale	$ 1,125.00	$ 855.00	$ 630.00	$ 450.00
Amount of buy-down	$ 400.00	$ -	$ -	$ -
Actual option profit	$ 725.00	$ 855.00	$ 630.00	$ 450.00
Option profit	$ 725.00	$ 855.00	$ 630.00	$ 450.00
Upside profit	$ -	$ 100.00	$ 600.00	$ 1,100.00
Total profit	$ 725.00	$ 955.00	$ 1,230.00	$ 1,550.00
Cost of shares	$ 9,000.00	$ 9,400.00	$ 9,400.00	$ 9,400.00
Return On Option (ROO)	8.1%	9.1%	6.7%	4.8%
Return on Upside	0.0%	1.1%	6.4%	11.7%
Total return	8.1%	10.2%	13.1%	16.5%
Annualized return	75.8%	95.5%	122.6%	154.4%

Figure 64

Procedure:

Simply input the information required into the top box of this page. All these figures are gleaned from the options chain.

Information Generated:

For each strike price submitted, the calculator specifies ROO (return on option), upside potential, downside protection, share buy down (I-T-M strikes), proceeds, cost basis and annualized returns. All of this information appears in a split second and can be printed to facilitate the best possible investment decisions. For example, in figure 64, one may opt for the 90 Call in a questionable market environment. This way, in addition to a fabulous 8.1% 39-d return, we are also receiving 4.3% of downside protection. In a more favorable market scenario, we may opt for a more aggressive 100 Call with a lower ROO (6.7%) but a tremendous upside potential (6.4%).

Multiple Tab

RETURN ON OPTION (ROO) CALCULATOR - MULTIPLE STOCKS

Stock Name or Symbol	Stock $/sh	Option $/sh	Strike $	Expires	Intrisic	Upside	ROO	Up Potential	Down Protect
hcbk (khq-kw)	$ 17.34	$ 1.00	$ 17.50	11/21/08	$ -	$ 0.16	5.8%	0.9%	0.0%
gild (gdq-kv)	$43.03	$ 2.70	$ 42.50	11/21/08	$ 0.53	$ -	5.1%	0.0%	1.2%
gild (gdq-ki)	$ 43.03	$ 1.60	$ 45.00	11/21/08	$ -	$ 1.97	3.7%	4.6%	0.0%
gis (gis-km)	$ 64.73	$ 3.00	$ 65.00	11/21/08	$ -	$ 0.27	4.6%	0.4%	0.0%
chtf (hqt-kn)	$ 67.35	$ 3.50	$ 70.00	11/21/08	$ -	$ 2.65	5.2%	3.9%	0.0%
nke (nke-kk)	$ 57.48	$ 5.20	$ 55.00	11/21/08	$ 2.48	$ -	4.9%	0.0%	4.3%
nke (nke-ki)	$ 57.48	$ 2.60	$ 60.00	11/21/08	$ -	$ 2.52	4.5%	4.4%	0.0%

Figure 65

Procedure:

Enter the required information in the left 5 columns. Once again, all these statistics are gleaned from the options chain.

Information Generated:

This is the tab that I use the most. When deciding on which financial soldiers you will send out into the investment battlefield for a particular month, this page allows you to compare a myriad of stocks and their corresponding potential option returns, upside potential and downside protection. In this example (figure65) one glance of the page will show us the option sales with the greatest returns, highest upside potential or best downside protection. We then make our decisions based on market tone and technical analysis. Please remember that what may seem like a burdensome task to master will become second nature to you over time. *If you've reached this point in the book, you have the intellect and motivation to succeed.*

What Now Tab

Rolling Out and Up: Out-of-The-Money

Roll Out
Roll Out + Up - Out-of-The-Money

WHAT SHOULD I DO NOW?

Stock name >>	FREEPORT MC-MORAN			
Stock symbol >>	fcx	Stock purchase price >>	$	78.00
# of shares owned >>	100	Stock price today >>	$	83.00
The expiring option is >>	fcx MAY 80.00			

	Symbol	Strike Price	Exp Date	Price / share
Roll out >>	fcx-yx	80.00	06/20/08	6.00
Roll out and up >>	fcx-yy	85.00	06/20/08	4.20
Roll out and down >>				

Old Wall Street adage: "Never try to catch a falling knife."
If the stock is out-of-the-money buy it back and find a better stock.
If the stock is in-the-money let it get called and find another stock.

THE CALCULATIONS BELOW DO NOT
INCLUDE BROKER COMMISSIONS.

COMPARE THESE RETURNS TO OTHER STOCK/OPTION
COMBINATIONS. THERE MAY BE A BETTER INVESTMENT.

WHAT IF I LET THE STOCK GET CALLED AWAY?
Do not count last month's return again.

Your proceeds from the expiring option premium were:	$	320.00
Your stock basis (for comparison) today would be:	$	8,000.00

The basis of the stock appearing on this page is for comparison purposes ONLY. It is the lower of the expiring option strike price or the current stock price. If you allowed the stock to be called away the amount you would have to invest on Monday is the proceeds. DO NOT USE THE FIGURES BELOW FOR TAX PURPOSES.

WHAT IF I ROLL OUT?

		w/o upside pot.
The proceeds for 1 fcx JUN 80.00 is:	$	600.00
The cost to buy back 1 fcx MAY 80.00 is:	$	(310.00)
Your net return will be:	$	290.00
Your comparative basis in the stock is:	$	8,000.00
Your comparative returns are:		3.63%
You downside protection is:		$300.00

WHAT IF I ROLL OUT AND UP?

		w/upside pot.		w/o upside pot.
The proceeds for 1 fcx JUN 85.00 is:	$	420.00	$	420.00
The cost to buy back 1 fcx MAY 80.00 is:	$	(310.00)	$	(310.00)
Your net profit on this option position is:	$	110.00	$	110.00
The "bought up" value in the closing option is:	$	300.00	$	300.00
Your upside potential return is:	$	200.00		
Your net return will be:	$	610.00	$	410.00
Your comparative basis in the stock is:	$	8,000.00	$	8,000.00
Your comparative returns are:		7.63%		5.13%
You downside protection is:				$0.00

Figure 66

Procedure:

Enter the information in the top box, obtained from the options chain. In the example in figure 66, the stock was originally purchased for $78 per share with the $80 Call sold. On or near expiration Friday the current market value of this equity was $83.

Information Generated:

1. The ROO obtained and downside protection if you roll out.

2. the ROO without upside potential when rolling out and up to an out-of-the-money strike.

3. The ROO with upside potential when rolling out and up to an out-of-the-money strike.

4. Highlights enhanced value via *buying up* the value of your shares (your neighbor moves from the kitchen into your dining room).

What Now Tab

Rolling Out and Up: In-The-Money

Roll out + up - in-the-money

WHAT SHOULD I DO NOW?

Stock name >>	FREEPORT MC-MORAN		
Stock symbol >>	fcx	Stock purchase price >>	$ 78.00
# of shares owned >>	100	Stock price today >>	$ 86.00
The expiring option is >>	fcx MAY 80.00		

	Symbol	Strike Price	Exp Date	Price / share
Roll out >>	fcx-yx	80.00	06/20/08	6.00
Roll out and up >>	fcx-yy	85.00	06/20/08	4.20
Roll out and down >>				

Old Wall Street adage: "Never try to catch a falling knife."
If the stock is out-of-the-money buy it back and find a better stock.
If the stock is in-the-money let it get called and find another stock.

THE CALCULATIONS BELOW DO NOT INCLUDE BROKER COMMISSIONS.

COMPARE THESE RETURNS TO OTHER STOCK/OPTION COMBINATIONS. THERE MAY BE A BETTER INVESTMENT

WHAT IF I LET THE STOCK GET CALLED AWAY?
Do not count last month's return again.

Your proceeds from the expiring option premium were:	$ 320.00
Your stock basis (for comparison) today would be:	$ 8,000.00

The basis of the stock appearing on this page is for comparison purposes ONLY. It is the lower of the expiring option strike price or the current stock price. If you allowed the stock to be called away the amount you would have to invest on Monday is the proceeds. DO NOT USE THE FIGURES BELOW FOR TAX PURPOSES.

WHAT IF I ROLL OUT?   w/o upside pot.

The proceeds for 1 fcx JUN 80.00 is:	$ 600.00
The cost to buy back 1 fcx MAY 80.00 is:	$ (610.00)
Your net return will be:	$ (10.00)
Your comparative basis in the stock is:	$ 8,000.00
Your comparative returns are:	-0.13%
You downside protection is:	$600.00

WHAT IF I ROLL OUT AND UP?   w/upside pot.   w/o upside pot.

The proceeds for 1 fcx JUN 85.00 is:	$ 420.00	$ 420.00
The cost to buy back 1 fcx MAY 80.00 is:	$ (610.00)	$ (610.00)
Your net loss on this option position is:	$ (190.00)	$ (190.00)
The "bought up" value in the closing option is:	$ 500.00	$ 500.00
Your upside potential return is:	$ -	
Your net return will be:	$ 310.00	$ 310.00
Your comparative basis in the stock is:	$ 8,000.00	$ 8,000.00
Your comparative returns are:	3.88%	3.88%
You downside protection is:		$100.00

Figure 67

Procedure:

Enter the information in the top box, obtained from the options chain. In the example in figure 67, the stock was purchased originally for $78 per share with the $80 Call sold. On or near expiration Friday the current market value of this equity was $86.

Information Generated:

1. The ROO obtained and downside protection if you roll out.

2. The ROO without upside potential when rolling out and up to an in-the-money strike. **There is no upside potential with an in-the-money strike.**

3. Highlights enhanced value via *buying up* the value of your shares (your neighbor moves from the kitchen into your dining room).

4. Provides you with a contract dollar amount of downside protection which is equivalent to the intrinsic value of the option. In this case, we are selling an $85 Call with the current market value of the stock @ $86. Therefore, we have $1 per share or $100 per contract of downside protection. In other words, if our shares do not decline by more than $100 per contract, our 3.88% 1-month return will be safe.

Utilization of this amazing tool will both expedite and enhance your investment decisions.

For a FREE Copy of the Ellman System Options Calculator

Contact me at alan@thebluecollarinvestor.com

For a FREE Introductory CD, join my mailing list:
http://www.thebluecollarinvestor.com/joinlist.shtml

To read my journal articles:
http://www.thebluecollarinvestor.com/blog/

For additional educational products, visit my store@
http://www.thebluecollarinvestor.com/store.shtml

Owen Sargent can be contacted @(osargentcpa@aol.com) to answer any questions relating to the calculator or tax consequences from options trading.

Fourteen

Concluding Remarks and Personal Observations

As I compose this chapter, I think back to when I first sat down to write this book. So many Blue Collar Investors asked me for more information on this subject, but the question remained; did I have enough material for a book. I thought about the small size of the universe of subject material I would be restricted to. This is not a book about investing, that's too broad a subject. Nor is this book about the stock market, stock options or covered call options. I already wrote that book! This is a book about exit strategies, a limited aspect of covered call writing. I knew that I wasn't addressing exit strategies for other types of investments, just covered call writing. Although I had my doubts about completing this book, you motivated me to sit down and give it a try. I entered the world of Microsoft Word and started typing. Once my fingers started getting sore I knew that this would be a successful mission.

As with all other aspects of our *cashing in on covered calls system,* no rocket science background is required. First we start with some basic knowledge: definitions; understanding why exit strategies are so important; grasping the math behind the 1-month contract; learning how to evaluate the key parameters; preparing your portfolio manager watch list; learning how to execute exit strategy trades and using the ESOC. After attaining a comfort level with the system, our focus turns to making money. We use our knowledge and common sense to achieve our goals of becoming CEOs of our own money and, ultimately, financial independence.

People will tell us everyday what we can't do, but they will never suggest what we are capable of doing. If you have read this book, you are no doubt motivated, and simply put, a cut above the rest. Your time could have been spent on the couch with a bag of chips, living your lives through singers, dancers, athletes or other celebrities. Instead you chose to spend your time educating yourself by reading my book.

Investing with stock options is not for everyone; a learning curve and a time commitment is required. Once you've educated yourself about covered call writing, only you can make the determination if investing with stock options is for you. Even if you choose not to sell covered call options, the education and perspective I offer can only make you a better investor, just as your feedback improves me as an investor. To our education system that didn't teach us about investing when we were in school, I say *it's time to spread the word.* The future Blue Collar Investors of the world need you to provide this information. To the naysayer who tells us what we can't do, I say, *I'll talk to you later when I return from the bank.* To all my fellow Blue Collar Investors who inspired me to write this book, I say, *thank you for your motivation, I loved every minute of it!*

Appendix I

Master Figure List of Charts and Graphs

Appendix II

My First Book, *Cashing in on Covered Calls*

Table of Contents

Appendix III

Articles Published in 2008
www.thebluecollarinvestor.com/blog

- How a Blue Collar Investor Manages a Volatile Market
- Dealing with Volatile Markets: The Media Experts vs. The Blue Collar Investor
- Stock Splits and their Effects on your Option Contracts
- Recession and Stagflation- How do we Respond?
- The Fall of Bear Stearns and the Lessons Learned
- Using Stock Options to Neutralize Negative Cash Flow Properties
- Short Selling: Good or Bad for the Stock Market?
- Jim Cramer Makes Us Some "Blue Collar Money" Volumes I-IX by Tony Covino
- Should I Buy that Stock? There is Only One Person Who Knows the Answer
- Being CEO of Your Own Money Means Making Informed Decisions

- Rising Oil Prices Create Blue collar Opportunities

- An Energy Plan that Makes Sense

- The Factors that Determine the Value of your Option Premium

- Earnings Reports are Telling us to Buy Stocks

- When to Buy Back your Option: Expiration Friday Dilemma

- Overnight Millionaire or Victim of the Rig?

- Locating Stock Gems from the IBD Homepage

- Warren Buffett Analyzes the Economy

- Hedge Funds and their Effect on our Investments

- The Mystery of Corporate Bonds

- Commingling of Asset Classes

- A Ridiculous Subprime Fairytale

- Mutual Funds: The Answer in these Volatile times?

- Blue Collar Investor Q&A

- Macroeconomics: The Governments Influence over our Investment Success

- A Day in the Life of a Stock investor

- Meet the Greatest Subprime Comedians

- Recession: A Normal Part of the Business Cycle

- Starbucks Saves a Life: A Holiday Feel-good Story

- The New York Stock Exchange: Part of a Global Conglomerate and a Stock to Watch

- Call to the SEC: Wake Up and Reinstate the Uptick Rule NOW

- The Bernie Madoff Ponzi Scheme: A Validation of our Blue Collar Philosophy
- An Historic Economic Reality Giving Birth to a New Generation of Investors

Appendix IV

Resource Center

Stock Research & Information - Free Web Sites:

1. The Blue Collar Investor: www.thebluecollarinvestor.com

2. http://finance.yahoo.com/

3. http://www.cnbc.com/

4. http://money.cnn.com/

5. http://www.fool.com/

6. http://www.marketwatch.com/

7. http://moneycentral.msn.com/investor/StockRating/srsmain. asp

Stock Research & Information– Paid Sites:

1. http://www.investools.com/

2. http://www.investors.com/

Glossary/Definitions - Free Web Sites:

1. http://stockcharts.com/school/doku.php?id=chart_school:glossary_a

2. http://www.zacks.com/help/glossary/?id=v_z&PHPSESSID=c761

3. http://www.cboe.com/LearnCenter/Glossary.aspx

4. http://www.investopedia.com/terms/o/optionchain.asp

Technical Analysis Charts

1. http://stockcharts.com/index.html

2. http://finance.yahoo.com/charts

Earnings Reports Information:

1. http://biz.yahoo.com/research/earncal/today.html

2. http://www.earningswhispers.com/

Stock Split Information:

1. http://biz.yahoo.com/c/s.html

2. http://www.investmenthouse.com/

Stock Screens:

1. http://moneycentral.msn.com/investor/finder/predefstocks.aspx

2. http://screener.finance.yahoo.com/newscreener.html

Options Information:

1. http://www.cboe.com/

2. http://www.888options.com/

Online Brokerage Web Sites:

1. www.usaa.com (military affiliation required as of 8/1/07)

2. www.thinkorswim.com

3. http://www.tdameritrade.com/welcome1.html

4. http://www.optionsxpress.com

5. http://www.scottrade.com/

Financial Newspapers/Magazines:

1. Investors Business Daily: www.investors.com

2. Wall Street Journal: www.wallstreetjournal.com

3. Barrons Weekly: www.barrons.com

4. Forbes magazine: www.forbes.com

Bonds Online Account and Information:

1. www.treasurydirect.gov

Mutual Fund/Exchange-Traded Fund Information

1. www.vanguard.com

Books/Suggested Reading

1. *One Up On Wall Street,* Peter Lynch

2. *Common Sense on Mutual Funds,* John C. Bogle

3. *Jim Cramer's Real Money,* James J. Cramer

4. *Jim Cramer's Mad Money,* James J. Cramer

5. *The Road to Wealth,* Suze Orman

6. *Getting Started in Options,* Michael C. Thomsett

7. *New Insights on Covered Call Writing,* Richard Lehman and Lawrence G. McMillan

8. *Fundamentals of the Options Market,* Michael S. Williams and Amy Hoffman

9. Cashing in on Covered Calls, Alan G Ellman (I really like this one the best!)

Appendix V

Testimonials

Since I published my first book, *Cashing in on Covered Calls*, I have received so many kind and generous letters and emails complimenting my book and system. I've read and appreciate every one of them. Sometimes I'll get constructive criticism which I also value as I use this information to enhance my articles, seminars, and books. It was actually this type of commentary that inspired me to write this book. I thank you for taking the time to contact me because when you have an important idea to enhance our investment decisions, I can pass it on to the community of all Blue Collar Investors. The following are highlights from some of those testimonials:

> GREAT BOOK!!!
>
> —Dr. B. Germany

> Your book and especially your DVDs explaining your methodologies & exit strategies are really outstanding....
>
> —Ken Y. Riverside, CA

> I am having such fun with (your system) it! And making money at that....
>
> —Jean K. Hacienda Heights, CA

Your book was very readable and very logical....

—Jim B. Blufton, SC

A must read book, very useful and information that can be implemented successfully.

—Robert E.

I enjoyed the CDs. Your system is great. I have averaged a little over 3.2% each month........

—Robert B. Flagstaff, AZ

Your approach is extremely refreshing. You actually use common sense....

—Robert G. Seabrook, NH

I was looking to get into the US markets. Your book has opened that door which is really exciting...

—Peter F. Australia

Thank you for your wonderful system. Sharing is caring.

—David S. Forest Hills, NY

Your book is great...

—Jim B. Perris, CA

Your book is easy to read, interesting, and best of all, I am applying the knowledge already.

—Cathy F. Towson, MD

I really enjoyed the seminars. What a wealth of information.

—Todd M. Commack, NY

Your book helped me understand the process much better than anything else I read.

—Patrick M. Denver, CO

I am very glad that I bought your book. Thanks.

—David Z. Mount Sinai, NY

Your book did a lot more to inspire me than any other book I've ever read or seen on a book shelf at Borders.

—David T. Overland Park, KS

Your book was one of the easiest reads on trading stocks and options outlining covered calls.

—Robert D. Nashville, TN

Thanks!! Your book is great.

—Gerald D. Bowling Green, KY

It is great, easy understanding, precise concept and principle.

—Brenda T. Hong Kong

I enjoyed the book and appreciate your weekly articles as well.

—Kyle A. New York, NY

I especially enjoyed 2 topics: Stock Selection and When to write a cc.

—Sam T. Birmingham, AL

I found your book very helpful and actually enjoyable reading.

—Steve D. Palm Beach Gardens, FL

I loved your book so much I ordered it for my former partner in the NYPD.

—Jason B. Belle Harbor, NY

Your writing and services are truly a breath of fresh air.

—Barry B. Jackson, NJ

I read your book and was very impressed with it.

—John H. Long Beach, CA

You have expertly described how to use this strategy.

—Dr. David S. Bartlett, NH

Thank you so much for sharing your experience.

—Don T. Leawood, KS

To those of you who wrote these testimonials and those who did not have your contact included in this appendix, I thank you so much for taking the time to inspire this author even more.

Appendix VI

Quick Start Form

I. Buy Monday Edition of Investors Business Daily – Section B

- Circle all stocks with an "o" next to the price. These are optionable stocks.

USE STOCK WATCH LIST LOCATOR FORM FOR II, III, and IV***

II. Go to www.investors.com and log in.

- Type in stock ticker.
- Highlight "get quote."
- Click on the magnifier icon.
- This will take you to the stock quote page where you will scroll down below the chart to the SmartSelect Ratings.
- Select only those stocks with six green circles under the "checklist" heading.

III. Go to http://moneycentral.msn.com/investor/StockRating/srs-main.asp

- Accept only stocks with a Scouter Rating of 5 or better.

IV. Go to www.stockcharts.com

- Set up chart as per figure 28 in Cashing in on Covered Calls.

- Accept only those equities with a favorable chart pattern.

V. Place all stocks remaining from screening process onto a **watch list**.

VI. Go to http://biz.yahoo.com/research/earncal/today.html or www.earningswhispers.com

Access ER dates and avoid those companies reporting during the current contract period.

VII. Use **option calculator (ESOC)** to determine return on option (ROO), upside potential, and downside protection, *when ready to sell options.*

VIII. Select an appropriate number of stock/option combinations based on available cash. Make sure you are well diversified with at least 5 stocks in different industries.

IX. Fill out *Form to Take to Computer* before actually buying stock and selling options.

X. Place all stocks purchased and options sold in your **portfolio manager.**

XI. Keep track of your monthly option profits in your **option log.**

XII. Be alert for possible **exit strategies**, especially if option value drops to 20% or 10% of original option premium sold.

Appendix VII

Pre-Expiration Friday Flow Chart
with <u>some</u> possible exit strategies

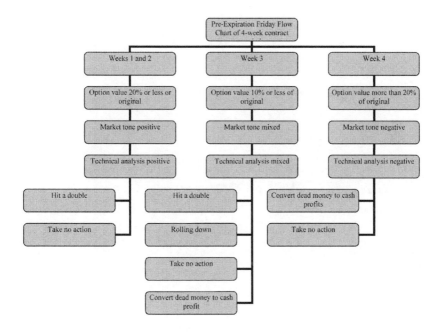

Appendix VIII

Expiration Friday Flow Chart
with <u>some</u> possible exit strategies

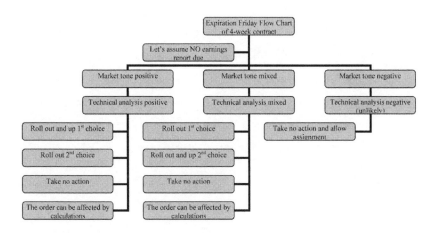

*Glossary

Accumulation: Buying of stock by institutional or professional investors over an extended period of time.

Acquisition: When one company purchases the majority interest in the acquired.

Actively Managed Mutual Funds: Shareholders, through a mutual fund manager, buy and sell stocks and bonds, within the fund, in an attempt to *beat the market.*

American Style Options: An option contract that may be exercised at any time between the date of purchase and the expiration date.

Ask: The price a seller is willing to accept for a security. It includes both price and quantity willing to be sold.

Assignment: The receipt of an exercise notice by an option seller that obligates him to sell (in the case of a call) or purchase (in the case of a put) the underlying security at the specified strike price.

At-the-money: An option is at-the-money if the strike price of the option is equal to the market price of the underlying security.

*Includes terms used in my first book, *Cashing in on Covered Calls*

Bearish: Pessimistic investor sentiment that a particular security or market is headed downward.

Bid: An offer made by an investor to buy an equity. It will include price and quantity.

Bullish: Optimistic investor sentiment that a particular equity or market will rise.

Buy down price of stock: Using the intrinsic value of an in-the-money option premium to reduce the cost of the stock purchase.

Buy to close: A term used by many brokerages to represent the closing of a short position in option transactions.

Call: An option contract giving the owner the right (but not the obligation) to buy a specified amount of an underlying security at a specified price within a specified time.

Convert Dead Money to Cash Profits: An exit strategy wherein an option is bought back and the underlying equity sold. The cash is then used to buy a better performing stock which is used to sell another covered call.

Cost basis: The original value of an asset. It is used to determine the capital gain, which is equal to the difference between the asset's cost basis and the current market value. Also: the amount of your original investment.

Covered call writing: A strategy in which one sells call options while simultaneously owning the underlying security.

Currency carry trade: A strategy in which an investor sells a certain currency with a relatively low interest rate and uses the funds to purchase a different currency yielding a higher interest rate. A trader using this strategy attempts to capture the difference between the rates, which can often be substantial, depending on the amount of leverage the investor chooses to use.

Dilution: A reduction in earnings per share of common stock that occurs through the issuance of additional shares. This is avoided with stock splits by reducing the current market value of a stock by a similar ratio as was the number of shares increased.

Distribution: the selling of stock by large institutions over an extended period of time.

Diversification: A risk management technique that mixes a wide variety of investments within a portfolio. The rationale behind this technique contends that a portfolio of different kinds of investments will, on average, yield higher returns and pose a lower risk than any individual investment found within the portfolio.

Dollar cost averaging: The technique of buying a fixed dollar amount of a particular investment on a regular schedule, regardless of the share price. More shares are purchased when prices are low, and fewer shares are bought when prices are high.

Downside protection: The intrinsic value portion of an in-the-money call option premium divided by the original cost basis. It is the percentage of your investment that can be lost without affecting the option return on your investment. The formula is as follows:

$$\frac{\text{Intrinsic Value of option premium}}{\text{Original Cost of stock}} = \% \text{ of downside protection}$$

Down trending Stock: A stock with a declining share price showing lower highs and lower lows.

Earnings estimate: An analyst's estimate for a company's future quarterly or annual earnings.

Earnings guidance: Information that a company provides as an indication or estimate of their future earnings.

Earnings report: A quarterly filing made by public companies to report their performance. Included in these reports are items such as net income, earnings per share, earnings from continuing operations, and net sales. These reports follow the end of each quarter. Most companies file in January, April, July, and October.

Earnings surprise: When the earnings reported in a companies quarterly or annual report are above or below analysts' earnings estimates.

ESOC: Ellman System Option Calculator which is an excel calculator used to compute option returns specifically for Alan Ellman's *Cashing In On Covered Calls* system.

ETFs: See exchange traded funds.

Exchange traded funds: A security that tracks an index, a commodity, or a basket of assets like an index fund, but trades like a stock on an exchange, thus experiencing price changes throughout the day as it is bought and sold. These securities provides the diversification of an index fund.

European Style Option: An option contract that can only be exercised on the expiration date.

Execution (of a trade): The completion of a buy or sell stock order.

Exit strategy: A plan in which a trader intends to get out of an investment position made in the past. It is a way of *cashing out or closing out a position.*

Expense ratio: A measure of what it costs an investment company to operate a mutual fund. It is determined through an annual calculation, where a fund's operating expenses are divided by the average dollar value of its managed assets Operating expenses are taken out of a fund's assets and lower the return to a fund's investors. Some funds have a marketing cost referred to as a 12b-1 fee, which would also be included in operating expenses. It is interesting that a fund's trading activity - the buying and selling of stock - is NOT included in the calculation of expense ratio.

Expiration date: The last day (in the case of an American- style) or the only day (in the case of European-style) on which an option may be exercised. For stock option, this date is the third Friday of the expiration month. If Friday is a holiday, the last trading day is the preceding Thursday.

Exponential moving average or EMA: A type of moving average that is similar to a simple moving average, except that more weight is given to the most recent data. It reacts faster to recent price changes than does a simple moving average. The 12- and 26-day EMA's are the most popular short-term averages, and they are used to create indicators like the MACD.

First call: A company that gathers research notes and earnings estimates from brokerage analysts and forms a consensus estimate. The estimate is compared to the actual earnings reports, and then the difference between the two is the earnings surprise. The other major player in this estimate game is **Zachs.**

Fundamental analysis: A method of analyzing the prospects of a security by observing the accepted accounting measures such as earnings, sales, and assets and so on.

Globalization: The tendency of investment funds and businesses to move beyond domestic and national markets to other markets around the globe, thereby increasing the interconnectedness of different markets. It has had the effect of increasing international trade and cultural exchange.

Hit a Double: An exit strategy wherein an option is bought back and then resold at a higher premium in the same contract period.

Hit a Triple: An exit strategy wherein an option is bought back and resold twice in the same contract period.

IBD 100: The Investor's Business Daily 100 is a computer-generated ranking of the leading companies trading in America. Rankings are based on a combination of each company's profit growth; IBD's Composite Rating, which includes key measures such as return on equity, sales growth and profit margins; and relative price strength in the past 12 months.

Index fund: A type of mutual fund with a portfolio constructed to mirror, or track, the components of a market index such as the S&P 500 Index. An index mutual fund is said to provide broad market exposure, low operating expenses and low portfolio turnover. *Indexing* is a passive form of fund management that has been successful in outperforming most actively managed mutual funds.

In-the-money: A term describing any option that has *intrinsic value*. A call option is in-the-money if the underlying security is higher than the strike price of the call.

Intrinsic value: The value of an option if it were to expire immediately with the underlying stock at its current price; the amount by which the stock is in-the-money. For call options, this is the positive difference between the stock price and the strike price.

Investor Fear Gauge: See **VIX.**

Key economic indicator: Macroeconomic data that is used by investors to interpret current or future investment possibilities and judge the overall health of an economy. These are specific pieces of data released by the government and non-profit organizations. These include:

The Consumer Price Index (CPI)
Gross Domestic Product (GDP)
Unemployment statistics
The price of crude oil

Lagging indicator: A technical indicator that trails the price action of an underlying asset. It is used by traders to generate transaction signals or to confirm the strength of a given trend. Since these indicators lag the price of the asset, a significant move will generally occur before the indicator is able to provide a signal. It confirms long-term trends but does not predict them.

Large cap: An abbreviation for the term *large market capitalization*. Market capitalization is calculated by multiplying the number of a company's outstanding shares by its stock price per share. The expression *large cap* is used by the investment community as an indicator of a company's size. A large cap stock has a market-capitalization dollar value of over 10 billion.

Limit Order: An order placed by a brokerage to buy or sell a specified number of shares at a specific price or better. The length of time an order remains outstanding can also be specified.

Long (position): The buying of a security, such as a stock or options contract, with the expectation that the asset will rise in value.

MACD (Moving average convergence divergence): A trend-following momentum indicator that shows the relationship between two moving averages of prices. The MACD is calculated by subtracting the 26-day exponential moving average (EMA) from the 12-day EMA. A 9-day EMA of the MACD, called the *signal line*, is then plotted on top of the MACD, functioning as a trigger for buy and sell signals.

MACD Histogram: A common technical indicator that illustrates the difference between the MACD and the trigger line. This difference is then plotted on a chart in the form of a histogram to make it easy for a trader to determine a specific asset's momentum.

Market capitalization: The total dollar market value of all of a company's outstanding shares. It is calculated by multiplying a company's shares outstanding by the current market price of one share. The investment community uses this figure to determine a company's size, as opposed to sales or total asset figures. Also referred to as *market cap*.

Market consensus: The average earnings estimates made by brokers and security analysts. Also known as *earnings expectations*.

Market Order: An order to buy or sell a stock at the current best available price.

Market Tone: The feeling of a market (general psychology) as demonstrated by the price activity of stocks. We use the VIX and S&P 500 chart patterns to help assess this sentiment.

Mergers: A general term used to refer to the consolidation of companies. It is a combination of two companies to form a new company.

Momentum indicator: Designed to track momentum in the price of a security to help identify the enthusiasm of buyers and sellers involved in the price trend development. Some indicators compare the closing price with some historical price so many periods before, others construct trend lines like the *MACD*. Others, like *Stochastics*, is a ratio using the high, low, and close values on various days.

Momentum Oscillator: A technical analysis tool that is banded between two extreme values and built with the results from a trend indicator for discovering short-term overbought or oversold conditions. As the value of the oscillator approaches the upper extreme value the asset is deemed to be overbought, and as it approaches the lower extreme it is deemed to be oversold. This oscillator is most advantageous when a stock price is in a trading range (sideways). An example is the *stochastic oscillator*

Money market securities: The securities market dealing in short-term debt and monetary instruments. These forms of debt mature in less than one year and are quite liquid. Treasury bills make up the bulk of the money market instruments. These securities are relatively risk-free.

Moving average: An indicator frequently used in technical analysis showing the average value of a securities price over a set period. Moving averages are generally used to measure momentum and define areas of possible support and resistance.

Multiple Tab of the ESOC: Compare returns, upside potential, and downside protection for many stocks, all on the same page.

Nasdaq 100 index: An index composed of the 100 largest, most actively traded U.S. companies listed on the Nasdaq stock exchange. This index includes companies from a broad range of industries with the exception of those that operate in the financial industry, such as banks and investment companies.

OHLC (bar) chart: Short for *Open High, Low Close chart*. This type of chart is used to spot trends and view stock movements, particularly on a short term basis.

Online Discount Broker: A stockbroker who carries out buy and sell orders online, at reduced commissions, but provides no investment advice.

Option: A contract that gives the owner the right, if exercised, to buy or sell a security or basket of securities (index) at a specific price within a specific time limit. Stock option contracts are generally for the right to buy or sell 100 shares of the underlying stock.

Option chain: A way of quoting option prices through a list of all the options for a given security. For each underlying security, the option chain tells investors the various strike prices, expiration dates, and whether they are calls or puts.

Options contract: Represents 100 shares in the underlying stock. Information included consists of the underlying security, type of option (call or put), expiration month, strike price and premium.

Option premium: The price at which the contract trades. It is the price paid by the buyer to the writer, or seller, of the option. In return the writer of the call option is obligated to deliver the underlying security to an option buyer if the call is exercised or buy the underlying security if the put is exercised. The writer keeps the premium whether or not the option is exercised.

Out-of-the-money: A call option is out-of-the-money if the strike price is greater than market value of the underlying security.

Over-the-counter option (OTC): An option traded off-exchange, as opposed to a *listed* stock option. The OTC option has a direct link between buyer and seller, has no secondary market, and has no standardization of strike prices and expiration dates. This securities market is not geographically centralized like the trading floor of the NYSE. Trading takes place through a telephone and computer network.

Overbought: A technical condition that occurs when prices are considered too high and susceptible to decline. Overbought conditions can be classified by analyzing the chart pattern or with indicators such as the Stochastic Oscillator. Generally, a security is considered overbought when the Stochastic Oscillator exceeds 80. Overbought is not the same as being *bearish. It simply infers that the stock has risen too far too fast and might be due for a pullback.*

Oversold: A technical condition that occurs when prices are considered too low and ripe for a surge. Oversold conditions can be classified by analyzing the chart pattern or with indicators such as the Stochastic Oscillator. Generally, a security is considered oversold if the Stochastic Oscillator is less than 20. Oversold is not the same as being *bullish. It merely infers that the security has fallen too far too fast and may be due for a reaction rally.*

Paper trade: A hypothetical trade that does not involve any monetary transactions. It is a risk-free way to learn the ins and outs of the market.

Passive management (of mutual funds): An investment strategy that mirrors a market index and does not attempt to beat the market.

Portfolio management: The art and science of making decisions about investment mix and policy, matching investments to objectives, asset allocation, and balancing risk versus performance. *It requires organized lists of accurate information.*

Price bar: see *OHLC*.

Put: An option contract that gives the holder the right, but not the obligation, to sell the underlying security at a specified price for a certain fixed period of time.

QQQQ: This is the ticker symbol for the Nasdaq 100 Trust, which is an exchange traded fund (ETF) that trades on the Nasdaq. It offers broad exposure to the tech sector by tracking the Nasdaq 100 index, which consists of the 100 largest non-financial stocks on the Nasdaq. It is also known as the *quadruple-Qs*.

Resistance: The price level at which there is a large enough supply of a stock available to cause a halt in the upward trend and turn the trend down. Resistance levels indicate the price at which most investors feel that the prices will move lower.

Rolling down: Closing out options at one strike price and simultaneously opening another at a lower strike price.

Rolling out (forward): Closing out of an option contract at a near-term expiration date and opening a same strike option contract at a later date.

Rolling up: Close out options at a lower strike and open options at a higher strike.

ROO (return on option): The percent profit realized from the sale of a covered call option based on the cost basis of the underlying stock. If an in-the-money option was sold, the intrinsic value is deducted from the option premium before calculating the return.

Rule of 72: A rule stating that in order to find the number of years required to double your money at a given interest rate, you divide the compound return into 72. The result is the approximate number of years that it will take for your investment to double.

S&P 500 (Standard and Poor's 500): An index consisting of 500 stocks chosen for market size, liquidity, and industry grouping, among other factors. It is designed to be a leading indicator of U.S. equities and is meant to reflect the risk/return characteristics of the large-cap universe.

Sarbanes-Oxley Act of 2002 (SOX): An act passed by the U.S. Congress to protect investors from the possibility of fraudulent accounting activities by corporations. It includes the establishment of a *Public Company Accounting Oversight Board* where public companies must now be registered.

Securities and Exchange Commission (SEC): A government commission, created by Congress, established to regulate the securities markets and protect investors. It also monitors the corporate takeovers in the U.S. The SEC is composed of five commissions appointed by the U.S. President and approved by the Senate. The statutes administered by the SEC are designed to promote full public disclosure and to protect the investing public against fraudulent and manipulative practices in the securities markets. Generally, most issues of securities offered in interstate commerce, through the mail or on the internet, must be registered with the SEC.

Sell to open: A phrase used by many brokerages on the street to represent the opening of a short position in option transactions.

Short (or short position): The sale (also known as *writing*) of an options contract or a stock to open a position.

Simple moving average (SMA): A moving average that gives equal weight to each day's price data.

Single Tab of the ESOC: Allows you to evaluate returns from different strikes for the same stock.

Stochastic Oscillator: A momentum indicator that measures the price of a security relative to the high/low range over a set period of time.

The indicator oscillates between 0 and 100. Readings below 20 are considered oversold. Readings above 80 are considered overbought.

StockScouter Rating: MSN Monet Central's rating of stocks from 1 to 10, with 10 being the best. It uses a system of advanced mathematics to determine a stock's expected risk and return.

Stock split: A change in the number of shares outstanding (in circulation). The number of shares are adjusted by the split ratio, e.g. 2 to 1. In this case, 1000 shares splits to 2000 shares but the opening price and current price are cut in half. The overall effect is to maintain the same cost and current value of an investment while increasing the number of shares and lowering the per share price. This makes it easier for small investors to own the stock in round lots.

Street expectation: The average earnings estimates made by brokers and security analysts.

Strike price: The stated price per share for which the underlying security may be purchased (in the case of a call) or sold (in the case of a put) by the option holder upon exercise of the option contract.

Support: A price level at which there is sufficient demand for a stock to cause a halt in a downward trend and turn the trend up. Support levels indicate the price at which most investors feel that prices will move higher.

Technical analysis: The method of predicting future stock price movements based on observation of historical stock price movements.

Time decay: A term used to describe how the theoretical value of an option *erodes* or reduces with the passage of time.

Time value: The portion of the option premium that is attributable to the amount of time remaining until the expiration of the option contract. Time value is whatever value the option has in addition to its intrinsic value.

Trading range: The spread between the high and low prices traded during a period of time.

Treasury note (one of the treasuries): A marketable, U.S. government debt security with a fixed interest rate and a maturity between one and ten years. T-notes can be bought either directly from the U.S. Government or through a bank.

Trend analysis: An aspect of technical analysis that tries to predict the future movement of a stock based on past data. It is based on the idea that what has happened in the past gives traders an idea of what will happen in the future. The concept is that moving with trends will lead to profits for the investor.

Trigger line / signal: Usually an exponential or simple moving average of a technical indicator which serves as a frame of reference for positive and negative divergences. For example, if the MACD indicator moves above its moving average, a bullish signal is produced.

Upside potential: Additional % of profit, as it relates to the underlying stock cost basis, that can be realized if the stock price reaches the strike price at expiration. It applies to out-of-the-money strike prices.

Uptrending Stock: A stock increasing in price with higher highs and higher lows.

Velocity (of money): A term used to describe the rate at which money is exchanged from one transaction to another.

VIX- CBOE Volatility Index: Demonstrates the market's expectation of a 30-day volatility. It measures market risk and is often referred to as the *investor fear gauge.*

Volume: The number of trades in a security over a period of time. On a chart, volume is usually represented as a histogram (vertical bars) below the price chart. The NYSE and Nasdaq measure volume differently. For every buyer, there is a seller: 100 shares bought = 100 shares sold.

The NYSE would count this as 100 shares of volume. However, the Nasdaq would count each side of the trade and as 200 shares volume.

Volume surge: An increase in the daily trading volume of an equity equal to at least 1.5 times its normal trading volume.

Watch list: A list of securities that are in consideration for investment buy/sell decisions.

What Now Tab of the ESOC: Calculates the returns for a package transaction where an option is bought back and another is sold.

Whisper number: The unofficial and unpublished earnings per share (EPS) forecasts that circulate among professionals on Wall Street. They were generally reserved for the favored (wealthy) clients of a brokerage.

Wilshire 5000 Total Stock Market Index: A market capitalization-weighted index composed of more than 6700 publicly traded companies. These companies must be headquarted in the U.S. and actively traded on an American stock exchange.

Yen carry trade: A strategy in which an investor sells the Japanese currency (yen) with a relatively low interest rate and uses the funds to purchase a different currency (dollar) yielding a higher interest rate. A trader using this strategy attempts to capture the difference between the rates-which can often be substantial, depending on the amount of leverage the investor chooses to use.

About the Author

Dr. Alan Ellman, author of best-selling *Cashing in on Covered Calls*, wears many hats during the course of a typical day. He is a licensed general Dentist in the State of New York and the owner of a vitamin store called The Natural Vitamin and Herb Source of Long Island. In addition to these titles, Alan is also a licensed certified Personal Fitness Trainer and a licensed Real Estate salesperson.

Alan is also an avid Real Estate Investor, owning properties in Texas, Florida, Pennsylvania and New York. He has often been invited to speak in front of large groups of investors about his successful investment properties.

Of all the facets of his life, Alan has become most passionate about the Stock Market and Call Options in particular. He loves the challenge of beating the market and sharing his ideas and system with others. This has manifest itself in the form of seminars and 1-on-1 coaching classes. In particular, he wants to spread the word about selling call options to the blue collar investor. Alan is determined to assist the average investor get the returns normally reserved for the Wall Street insiders.

Not only does Alan want you to achieve successful results in your stock market investing, he wants you to be in total control of the process. To learn how to best accomplish these goals and become CEO of Your Own Money, please visit his web site at **www.TheBlueCollarInvestor.com**.

Index

Made in the USA
San Bernardino, CA
09 December 2015